The Great Salt Lake Mime Saga and Amsterdam's Festival of Fools

Memoir and Memorabilia

by Michael R. Evans

Illustrated Edition

Photographs and Memorabilia

from The Road (1973-1984)

First Worldwide Printing
Revision I -- 2016

All images in this book are created from personal memorabilia donated by the author and participants in the events. Black and white quotations from programs were scanned from material distributed free to the general public, and are covered under Fair Use provisions of international law.

The Great Salt Lake Mime Saga and Amsterdam's Festival of Fools
Revision I

Copyright ©2016 by Michael R. Evans All Rights Reserved
ISBN: 978- 0- 692- 69628- 6

Front Cover: Digital adaptation of a Festival of Fools sticker adhered to the author's logbook from 1977. Artist: Gielijn Escher. Rear Cover: From a mounted poster in the residence of Matthew Child. Artist: Jan Jaap Dekker. Interior photographs and graphics contributed by Ted Van Zutphen, Ed Baker, Warwick Moreton, Davey Norket, Suzette Bronkhorst, Mark Nelson, Marion Onekink, Peter Domela Nieuwenhuis, Ellen Beier, Karen Quest, Patsy Droubay, Matthew Child, Stuart Curtis, and Gregg Moore. Images by Jan Jaap Dekker are used with the artist's permission. Framed posters courtesy of Matthew Child. All digital artwork and restoration by Michael R. Evans. Credit is given when known and contributions acknowledged whenever possible. Readers are encouraged to check out all the full-sized colorful artwork available from Gielijn Escher.

In Praise of Older Media

In an age of wireless digital media, it may seem odd to commit words and pictures to a medium that has been literally laying about since the late Middle Ages. However, one major reason we know as much as we do about the last seven centuries is the paper and ink printing process.

All media in the online world exist merely as coded patterns of electrons, stored on machines in unknowable locations around the globe and may only be decoded by other machines.

This solid object containing text and graphics may be held in a reader's hands. No electricity is required to operate a book. As long as there is enough light to see, there is light enough to read. This volume is easy to use in a variety of body positions, and easy to transport by various means. One may tackle the contents in any order, and the details will not change, for good or bad, when revisiting the material. These features remain in effect when loaned to friends. Given the right circumstances, my pretty little history book could endure for another seven centuries in its present form.

Hazards like fire and flood could damage pages or whole chapters, but what remains would still tell a story despite missing those elements. These conditions should be avoided, however, and regular timely replacement by purchasing more books is highly recommended.

On Idioms and Slang: The author utilizes references to contemporary radio, television, news stories, movies, music, literature, and art history to evoke the cultural atmosphere of those times. I also use slang liberally -- *Outta' State* was a popular malapropism derived from *out of sight*. The wonderfully English ... *under the cosh* is explained by its context. *In Search Of...* was an American TV show that featured Leonard Nimoy as host. There are many more, and my international readers are cordially invited to research any or all of them over the miraculous Internet.

First Worldwide Printing
Revision I -- © 2016
Media Man Productions

Dedicated to the people and city of Amsterdam.

CONTENTS

Foreword and Introduction	I
Early SLC Mime Troupe	14
SLC Mime Troupe; Year Two	18
1974 International Mime Festival	24
Great Salt Lake Mime Troupe	35
First Tour: Aspen Highlands	42
California Pt. 1	48
California Pt. 2	55
California Pt. 3	61
Coast to Coast to Europe	68
1975 Festival of Fools and Holland	79
Amsterdam's Festival of Fools	
1975 Festival of Fools	96
1976 Festival of Fools	99
1977 Festival of Fools	103
1978 Festival of Fools	106
1979 Festival On Tour	109
1980 Festival of Fools	111
1982 Festival Op Straat	113
1984 Festival Finale	116
Author's Notes and Afterword	120

The Great Salt Lake Mime Saga
and Amsterdam's Festival of Fools

Memoir and Memorabilia
by Michael Evans

Illustrated Edition
Photographs and Memorabilia
from The Road (1973-1984)

First Worldwide Printing
Revision I -- 2016

Foreword and Introduction

This memoir was originally published as an illustrated online project named The Great Salt Lake Mime Troupe Saga, which further branched off to trace the career-arcs of certain performers and companies associated with Amsterdam's Festival of Fools. These artists created work that transcended decades and continents, and might fill an encyclopedia rather than this modest history and reminiscence.

Amsterdam's Festival of Fools was the emotional climax of the Great Salt Lake Mime Troupe's journey from the University of Utah to Colorado, California, and across the ocean to the Netherlands, where they found audiences that appreciated their comedy, music, and dance. The Festival of Fools continued on through the Seventies and into the Eighties.

I decided to structure the last sections of this book keyed on Amsterdam's Festival of Fools because the Great Salt Lake Mime Troupe metamorphosed, then split up permanently. I also moved back to the USA. The complete programs are online, documenting performers, places, and projects that occurred in and around Amsterdam and even further afield. (https://amsterdamfools.wordpress.com) The reader will repeatedly see the names of long-time Troupers and Fools who vigorously pursued their art across the blue horizons of Planet Earth. This book ends as the Festival of Fools ends, with the last gathering in 1984. For these reasons, I have extended the original title.

"Saga" is a story told by a storyteller, from the Germanic *sage* (sah-gah) "to say." There are some reprints from newspapers here and there, and a few quotes written by friends who were on the spot, but this theatrical tale is otherwise described from my vantage point as artistic ally and stage manager / technician for the Great Salt Lake Mime Troupe. The story focuses on events concerning the group's history as if they were seen through a video camera. Private affairs are left out as much as humanly possible, but I share some of my personal feelings at times.

This book contains most of the same text as the website, with revisions made for focus and clarity. Interior black and white illustrations consist of contemporary photographs whenever available -- with additional drawings by me, and a variety of memorabilia created over the years. Profuse thanks to Rembrandt Van Rijn for setting high standards in black ink and aquatints. This Illustrated Edition acts as a Valentine for the City of Amsterdam and commemorates the 40th anniversary of the first Festival of Fools.

Michael R. Evans
Amsterdam, Holland
February 14, 2015

The Great Salt Lake Mime Saga
and Amsterdam's Festival of Fools
Memoir and Memorabilia
by Michael R. Evans

Illustrated Edition
*Photographs and Memorabilia
from The Road (1973-1984)*

First Worldwide Printing
Revision I -- © 2016

The Early SLC Mime Troupe
SLC Mime Troupe; Modern Dance; RDT Workshop; and Theater 138.

Salt Lake City first sees and hears about the Mime Troupe

Jim Anderson (far left) Top Row: Evy Tessman, Patsy Droubay, and Stephanie the dancer.
Middle Row: Wendy Loring, Franklin Tomorrow, Matthew Child, and Jeff the film maker.
Bottom Row: Becky Bernson, Katie Apenzeller / Berger, Steve Rasmussen, and Paul Blackwell.

    Salt Lake City's *Deseret News* published Dave Conley's photo above and an article by Joe Bauman during June 1973 about Pantomine at Trolley Square -- a mall created from former bus garages. I started making videos with the Mime Troupe soon afterward -- they rehearsed in the gray concrete halls of the Art Department where I was attending classes at the University of Utah.
    As 1973 dawned, I took courses in TV production, plus my friend Al Payne arranged a video workshop from mutual friend Paul McCarthy, a former graduate student who was becoming a well-known conceptual artist. I made up my mind that I would redouble my efforts to escape the dirt and danger of my industrial job, moved into a studio near the University, and diligently went about taking photographs, drawing, and painting away from the school. Feeling a need to do something with potential for the future, I borrowed some money, drove to Los Angeles and picked up a new Sony Porta-Pack from McCarthy and his friend Mike Cram. I paid it off by staying on the midnight shift at Kennecott Copper Corporation, while still going for my degree at the University of Utah, and losing a lot of sleep.
    My studio was an absolute delight! It was fun being in close proximity to other people my own young age who were also learning about life. I looked around for appropriate subjects to videotape, and found plenty in the world of Modern Dance and Ballet, on campus, and also right next door to my art studio. I did some work with a professional model named Mary, a dancer who lived nearby. She introduced me to many creative people in her scene. I'd been learning how to draw and paint human figures, knowing

that it would be a long, hard process. By the time I rented the studio, I knew a few things but there was still so much more to learn. My devotion to figural art drew me to Modern Dance, Ballet, and Pantomime, all which employed the human body for expressions that were as profound as the best novels, poetry, movies, or visual imagery.

Videotaping at the University of Utah Dance Department

The first few months I spent shooting video and learning how to work behind a lens was more than just remarkable -- this time literally marked the beginning of the rest of my life.

The Mime Troupe consisted of talented, ambitious dancers -- some of the best on campus. Their material was well-thought out and extremely well-executed. I not only videotaped the Mime Troupe's rehearsals, but also recorded a beautiful Modern Dance piece for a graduate student's master thesis at the U of U's Dance Department, thanks to a friend named Lisa. I followed the Mime Troupe to their first gig at the Hidden Valley Country Club, and put their own concert at the Dance Building onto videotape.

Since I enjoyed the creative scene in the Dance Department, I signed up for Repertory Dance Theatre's 1973 Summer Workshop, where we delved deep into the intricacies of the new portable video medium and shot a full-scale RDT concert. I also made some ZenTV tapes on my own, and actually oil-painted on a TV screen, tweaked for video feedback, during our final presentation in the Architecture Building Gallery.

The Mime Troupe Continued to Attract Attention

I moved into another studio near Ninth East and Ninth South, an ongoing center of creativity in Salt Lake City, and shared the space with musician Curt Setzer. The Mime Troupe performed throughout the summer and fall of 1973 -- although several members came and went and new members joined too. It was fun to help them out, because my experiences with them were so instructive and positive, and their shows were so strong and delightful. They found new rehearsal space in the Music Building and did their second major concert on the orchestral stage there. Jim Anderson played King Claudius plus wrote much of the next performance at Westminster College. Dancer Amy Osgood played Queen Gertrude and choreographed pieces for herself and others.

The Mime Troupe Asserted Its Presence in the Community

The successful Music Building concert gave everybody a big lift during late summer. The Mime Troupe lost and gained some members to the vicissitudes of school and professional careers. Wendy Loring and Matt Child returned from the East Coast and Africa in the Autumn, though, and three persons showed up who would stay awhile -- David Carrillo from the U.S. Navy and SLC, Daniel Robert from New York, and Stuart Curtis from Michigan, who lent Paul Blackwell a much-needed hand with the music.

After an outdoor children's show at Westminster College, they scheduled their next big production at one of Salt Lake City's most prestigious venues -- Theater 138, founded by Ariel Ballif, Tom Carlin, and Stu Falconer at 138 South 200 East. (It was a parking lot by the time SLC hosted the 2002 Olympics.) They ran a first-rate place, and it was a high honor to perform there.

It was a magnificent show -- Paul and Stuart made a lot of music for two men; David helped Katie sing her own tune *Hilly Road*; Daniel Robert channeled a wistful Shakespeare; Evy, Katie, and 13-year-old Allison Mahaffey knocked 'em dead right way in the opening *Classroom* sequence; Chris, Patsy, Matthew, David, and Evy did increasingly better solos, which would lead to later larger works; and Wendy's madcap *Silhouettes On The Shade* left everybody laughing at the intermission. The second half was an ambitious domestic psychodrama that used everybody's vocal gifts and visual prowess, with an intense pantomime finale by Katie and Patsy that wrenched everyone's emotions. The whole evening was original and beautiful.

My friend and studio-mate Pat Eddington drew and painted many mimes and clowns the previous year. He graciously allowed me to reproduce one from his series for our show at Theatre 138.

I participated in this show on several levels -- not only printing a high-quality poster, but supplying microphones and other equipment. A Doo-Wop bass was needed for Wendy Loring's elaborate *Silhouettes* number so I appeared in a suit, greased-up hair, and sunglasses. The event needed to be videotaped at least once, but I couldn't BE in the show and SHOOT it at the same time, so I sacrificed a Friday night to crawl through the former window of an abandoned projection booth space above and behind the audience with my equipment. Somehow, the microphones weren't on, so I had to crawl out and back in as everybody was in their seats, waiting for the show to start. *(Hiya Lisa! Don't I look like a bloody fool?)* It never happened on any other night, or in rehearsal.

The SLC Mime Troupe briefly became SLC Mime Theatre

It was also time for a time-out for me as winter settled in ... I spent much more effort paying attention to my job, my other friends, and my private life. I was simply tired too, and didn't see anything I could contribute to the small gigs their manager set up for SLC Mime Theatre.

However, I kept contact with Katie, who shared a house with Paul, Stuart, and Daniel near the University. David, Patsy, and Matthew always showed up there too. The Tessmans lived a short walk away, but were too busy working and raising their two sons to act as Mime Central anymore -- they still threw some darn good parties, though!

I shot some small video experiments in the 9th and 9th studio, and even joined musicians Curt Setzer, Dave Faggioli, Neil Passy, Richard Jonas, and Rod Dankers for jam sessions once a week as the Nameless Uncarved Block -- I videotaped a couple of happenings with them and we worked with an actress/model named Linda. We were even on KMOR Radio once, but it was harmless fun rather than serious work, for me at least. However, some of my 'Block' companions at the radio station continued to bring hours of non-commercial music to the area for another decade and more.

Looking back, it seems odd that I didn't go out much socially with video model Linda, although we saw the great bluesman Willie Dixon performing at the University of Utah together. Matthew Child from the Mime Troupe sat with us, and a discussion about partnership in yet another new studio on Capitol Hill arose during the course of that fabulous evening of music.

I was frankly missing the various combinations of structured preparations and spontaneous performances I'd experienced in the Dance Department. The freewheeling 'Block' had been fun on the weekends, but music wasn't my profession. The Mime Troupe consisted of performers actually going somewhere with their careers, and that quirky little gimmick of Modern Dance mixed with Modern (Panto) Mime was their chosen vehicle. It became my own chosen vehicle too, and I was pleased to be asked to help them with my own barely-tested talents.

SLC Mime Troupe -- Year Two

Hillside Studio, University Ballet Department, Boogie Bar, and Disco Nights.

Building up -- The Mime Troupe lays down the necessary foundations for interstate and international exposure.

The Mime Troupe moved to the carriage house of the McCune Mansion on Capitol Hill. Our first few weeks in the Hillside Studio are still a blur in my memory. We were mostly involved with cleaning and painting a two story building that had been neglected for an indefinite number of years. Rehearsals, workshops, and jam sessions occurred, of course, becoming more frequent as the place got more presentable.

Our stage in the north side of the upper floor, inside the lovely Carriage House of Salt Lake's historic McCune Mansion. It was later razed for a parking lot. (Clockwise) Matthew Child, Stuart Curtis, Katie Appenzeller, David Carrillo, Evy Tessman, and Paul Blackwell.

I rejoined them and helped out by renting one of the studios in the building, along with Tom Tessman, plus my friend and classmate Sparry from the University of Utah's Art Department. Daniel Robert seriously took on the job of manager, and everything was done with a greater intensity.

There was an anteroom opening onto Hillside Avenue to the north, which led to a small stage, and then hundreds of square feet of sprung wooden floor on the top floor, along with a raised alcove at the south end, where we set the piano. A borrowed set of drums appeared one day, thanks to Dave Fagiolli of the Nameless Uncarved Block.

Downstairs had a washroom, a broom closet, and three artist's studios -- mine was farthest eastward, Tom's was in the middle, and Sparry's was nearest to the west door.

Since we were on a slope, we were able to walk in and out at ground level, and there was plenty of light. Sparry discovered a secret room behind her south wall, and lost no time opening the space. She made tea every evening and always visited me, cups in hand, when I was there. Tom's space became vacant after Evy left the group.

(Left to Right) Paul Blackwell, David Carrillo, Patsy Droubay, Katie Apenzeller, and Matthew Child rehearsing on the south side of Hillside Studio's upper level. Portions of the McCune Mansion (which still stands in 2016) are visible through the windows.

Hey -- get to work!   Is this WORK?   Sure -- it's work!

Matthew and Patsy were both well-trained dancers. They kept pace with Katie, and brought their own ideas. My main job with the Mime Troupe was videotaping classes and rehearsals, so that the dancers could see what was working -- and what wasn't. I also drew pictures, took photos, and created graphics for publicity purposes. Yes, I was still working nights at the engine house of a railroad located twenty miles away, but I slept in the mornings, and joined Katie and Paul for their classes midday in the Ballet Department at the University of Utah.

It felt great going to the University as a professional instead of as a student but I was also learning about my new chosen field from people who had been dancing since they were small children. Scary, but fun! Katie and Patsy also taught private classes at the Hillside Studio. In between these times, our dancers would work on creating new material while our musicians improvised or composed original music for the group.

***Music hath charms to soothe the savage breast, to soften rocks, or bend a knotted oak* -- William Congreve (1670–1729) in** *The Mourning Bride,* **Act I Scene 1**

Unlike any other dance company, we had our own live band. Paul Blackwell had been with the group since the beginning, and wrote original music. His friend Stuart Curtis moved all the way from Michigan in the late summer of 1973 to work with him.

Stuart was particularly talented on reed instruments like clarinet and saxophone. He played a powerful flute, and was a better than average pianist. David Carrillo came on board after serving time in the U.S. Navy. Blackwell played piano, guitar, and composed..We performed many times at Westminster College, a private university on the east side of Salt Lake City with Jazz in their music curriculum.

This was the SLC Mime Troupe's basic poster during early 1974 -- Clockwise from the top: David, Patsy, Katie, and Matthew. Photo shot on Hillside Avenue by Daniel's friend "Petey."

The Mime Troupe had a whole new professional focus, with a common goal of somehow creating a unique dance company, and making it succeed in the marketplace.. We were fortunate to have the personable but aggressive Daniel Robert to guide us and speak with artistic sponsors.

Daniel was alert to opportunities others surely would have missed in our motley crew. To the west of the Hillside studio was a high-rise apartment building where a big band musician from California named Hal Schaer resided. He heard Paul and Stuart play from his balcony, came over to visit them, and encouraged us all to persevere. He'd played with Bob Crosby's well-established orchestra and possessed high professional standards. Hal was a mentor to Stuart in particular, and they stayed friends for a decade or more until Curtis eventually moved away to Hamburg, Germany.

We faced a challenge in finding other musicians who could match Paul and Stuart's abilities, and would work for what little we were able to share -- jam sessions helped, plus the word of mouth that developed from them, and through the Dance Department grapevine. William Fowler and Ladd McIntosh had recently relocated their world-class Jazz program over to Westminster College, where Stuart took music courses, and made even more contacts.

We met talents like pianist John Fischer, bassist Mark Nelson, and local keyboard giant Stu Goldberg, who moved onward and upward with the Fowler Brothers. (Later, Katie choreographed a terrific dance to his beautiful song *Lotus Feet*.)   Eventually, we coaxed a high-energy hard-rock drum-and-bass rhythm section from journeyman guitarist James Warburton's 'Brother Music' into joining our band with the promise of work on the local bar scene.

The buzzword going around the artistic community happened to be THE BARS. There were a lot of them, and business was good, as thousands of Baby Boomers hit legal age and unleashed a tsunami of beer. Rod Dankers recruited many fellow Nameless Uncarved Block inmates into his own bar-band called Ragazine, and they remained a source of good advice on that front.

We kept our promise to Fred Watts and Bud Okubo -- the former played a double-sized drum kit, and the latter had new Peavy bass equipment. Our musicians all enjoyed playing unusual time signatures, and our dancers were inspired by their unconventional rhythms, plus found that it was easy (for them) to keep cues straight in odd time signatures like five over four and six over eight

After a baptism by fire at Big Joe's, a venue which really required an electric band, Daniel asserted we were ready to face the audience at Salt Lake City's most surprisingly successful watering hole -- The Sun Tavern, one of the first openly gay discos in the Western USA. Everyone who went there wanted something out of the ordinary, and that's what we were about to deliver!

Daniel was correct, as usual, The Sun attracted people from all walks of life, especially our audiences from the University and sundry alternative communities. The regulars came from mixed social strata, but they enjoyed good entertainment, no matter what their origins happened to be.

The patrons of the Sun were already used to theatrics, because the place presented frequent cabaret shows featuring impersonations of Marilyn Monroe and other High Camp heroines. The backbone of the tavern's business, was their LOUD sound system, and a collection of popular Soul Music that made everybody of every sex get on up and dance for hours on end -- refreshing themselves at the bar of course. The records I now recall the most included *Rock the Boat*, by The Hues Corporation; *Rock Your Baby* by George McCrae; *Kung Fu Fighting* by Carl Douglas, and *Jungle Boogie* by Kool and the Gang -- *Get Down! Get Down!* This kind of scene would soon be called Disco and sweep the globe. The Sun evolved from a row of railroad bars and commercial storefronts next to the Union Pacific Depot. It was once named the Railroad Exchange before local radio talk-show host Joe Redburn took over the place and eventually turned it into a popular dance club serving both mixed and gay customers.

The Mime Troupe's bar shows started with our company's strength -- dancing. The band worked up a special introduction that kicked into high gear after a few short measures, once the actors/dancers made their entrances. It was obvious to even the most jaded barflies that these people could MOVE. The characters and scenarios which tied the dances together were incisive, funny, and yet refreshingly respectful of humanity -- they were also brash and sexy, and the music was GOOD! The flame of High Culture burned brightly in the industrial slums around Salt Lake's rail yards -- among people who were looking for a good time, which included us.

The ideal of "theater for the people" was a reality, but so was the desperate side of night life -- the Dance world lost some great artists because of accidents in dark places. There are really inherent dangers in promiscuous "partying," and situations which should have been obvious to us all back then.

Theater -- was that some sort of a building, or something we actually DID?

A couple of well-established local venues presented Mime concerts in the spring of 1974 -- Canadian Claude St. Denis filled Kingsbury Hall, and proved that there was a significant audience for the art form. Menagerie Mime Theatre from San Francisco visited us at the U of U campus after a concert for BYU in Provo, Utah.

Although the SLC Mime Troupe eventually proved that we could compete with the vulgar noise of the urban/suburban street, it took a while before we mounted our own return to the conventional stage. Daniel enlisted the help of theatrical artists Ken and Barb White to assess our technical needs. Ken set up lights at ski resorts, taverns, and other places we wanted to play. Ken also trained me in the basics of being a theater technician and built an ingenious portable lighting system which we used for a year.

For quiet theater stages, our dancers adopted the characters of children playing gently. A whole world developed from their easily-perceived games. As the concert went on, they brought in various combinations of new material and scenarios from earlier shows, which were expanded over time, then refined by practice and integration with their on-stage bandmates.

An attentive audience in a darkened hall with proper lighting witnessed a greater range of dynamics and emotions than anything possible in the human hubbub of night spots. However, we acquired a certain edge from working in the latter places which was unobtainable by other means.

After months of development, we presented a new show in a venue our public didn't know, but we also scored big in our first out of state concert in Steamboat Springs, Colorado.

Instead of an established location, we took a chance on booking our Spring Concert at a perfectly fine space in Salt Lake's so-called Central City. After months of development, we presented our first full-scale independent concert, but in a venue almost totally unknown to the public. Our regular audience didn't follow us there either. The show was first-rate, but only few dozen people came. During this ordeal, Sparry took my hand one afternoon and dragged me to the Art Department Picnic in the cool green mountains, where she praised what we were doing at Hillside Studio for our classmates.

Daniel's hard work was not done in vain. -- The Mime Troupe impressed over half a thousand strangers at a show about five weeks later. We scored our first concert outside of Utah at an Arts Festival in Steamboat Springs, Colorado after we were finished with Sumner School. They gave us nice accommodations at a golf course condo and moved us into the closing spot that evening, following a one-act play. Our performance was advertised simply as a Dance Concert and rightly so -- Salt Lake Mime Troupe was always a Dance Company.

1974 International Mime Festival

La Crosse the mighty Mississippi -- Europe, Asia, and the Communist Bloc.

SLC Mime Troupe -- Meeting the World

Summary: The Salt Lake Mime Troupe took over the carriage house of the McCune Mansion on Capitol Hill as 1973 became 1974. We also took on a new professionalism, or at least tried. I assisted Katie and Paul at University Utah by videotaping them and their students. She and Patsy also taught workshops at the Hillside Studio. The front door of our sturdy carriage house was on Hillside Avenue.

Daniel Robert, our friend and manager from New York, took a couple of bold steps on our behalf -- he booked us at the Sun Tavern, one of the first openly gay discos in Salt Lake, or the Western USA. Everyone who went there liked to see something out of the ordinary, and they loved our show!

We first worked out of state in Steamboat Springs, Colorado during the spring, and Daniel decided to send Matthew Child, Katie, Dave Carrillo, and Patsy Droubay to La Crosse, Wisconsin for the International Mime Festival and Institute.

Left to Right: Matthew Child, David Carrillo, Katie Apenzeller, and Patsy Droubay posing outside the McCune mansion's carriage house off Hillside Avenue.
Photograph by Daniel Robert's friend Pete.

During one of Katie's movement workshops in May, a Kindergarten teacher named George Kugler from Seattle, Washington showed up after reading one of our brochures. He was a tall, strong, bearded man with a gentle disposition and a fierce eagerness to learn. He enjoyed Katie's classes so much that when he read about the International Mime Festival he registered by mail and took off for the Midwest, where we saw him later that summer.

I made one of the most important personal decisions of my life when I gave up my industrial job to follow our dancers to La Crosse along with our new band. As mentioned previously, Paul Blackwell and Stuart Curtis joined forces with a hard-rocking drummer and a proficient bass player. They enjoyed mixing up time-signatures, and our dancers enjoyed the new rhythms. Our customers in the bars liked their music LOUD, and our band delivered the high-decibel goods.

The International Mime Festival was a total trip -- we drove my red Volkswagen over the Wasatch Mountains into Wyoming. We then roared on into the night through Nebraska and Iowa while the Northern Lights glimmered in the blue-black skies to our left. After a short sleep in an Iowa field, we drove among the islands of the upper Mississippi to the Wisconsin Dells, where we descended down a high bridge into La Crosse and found Viterbo College which hosted the event.

We asked around and found Matthew, Katy, Patsy, and David at a lecture-demonstration featuring Dimitri the famous Swiss clown, moderated by Bari Rolfe. He had been scheduled to leave that week but remained throughout the whole festival. He even performed a second show because so many people wanted to see him perform again. Dimitri communicated quite well in English and his wife was along to help him out too, but he had no trouble talking with anybody. He was bright, open, friendly, and flashed the widest smile in the entire world.

The dancers made room for us in the dormitory, and the rest of the first day was a blur of getting acquainted with the other participants, and sleeping off the weariness of a thousand-mile dash in my rather small Volkswagen. It didn't take too long to discover that La Crosse was the home of the Heileman Breweries and that there were more bars and liquor stores than any other type of business in that little town.

A particularly large club on Main Street featured live music every night, and I found myself down there the next evening dancing with a proper, sophisticated Japanese lady named Mamako Yoneyama, who was regarded as an Eastern Goddess among Mime professionals. She enjoyed hearing everybody's stories about where we came from, and our dreams and goals. If you didn't fall in love with Mamako just a little, then you never met her. She made friends with everyone she met. When we all crowded into the main theater to see her, Mamako began her stage performance singing a nightclub song in English, then continued on to silently satirize oxygen masks, Tokyo, modern subways, and finally wove an epic pantomimed fairy tale in a long solo dance.

Another friendly individual named Antonin Hodek was from Czeckoslovakia. He walked right up to me while I was packing my camera, and told me of photos he had shot on his journey between Los Angeles and La Crosse. Two of them were significant to me as well -- a wild white horse in Wyoming, and an angelic beam of light from the clouds over Salt Lake City. (I showed him a drawing of the flat farmlands of Nebraska.)

The next significant episode I remember was a showing of *Les Enfants du Paradis (Children of Paradise)* in the main theater. Jean-Louis Barrault was outstanding as Jean Baptiste Deburau, the man who turned "Pierrot" from an obscure white faced Commedia Dell 'Arte character into a popular and ubiquitous icon during the 19th Century.

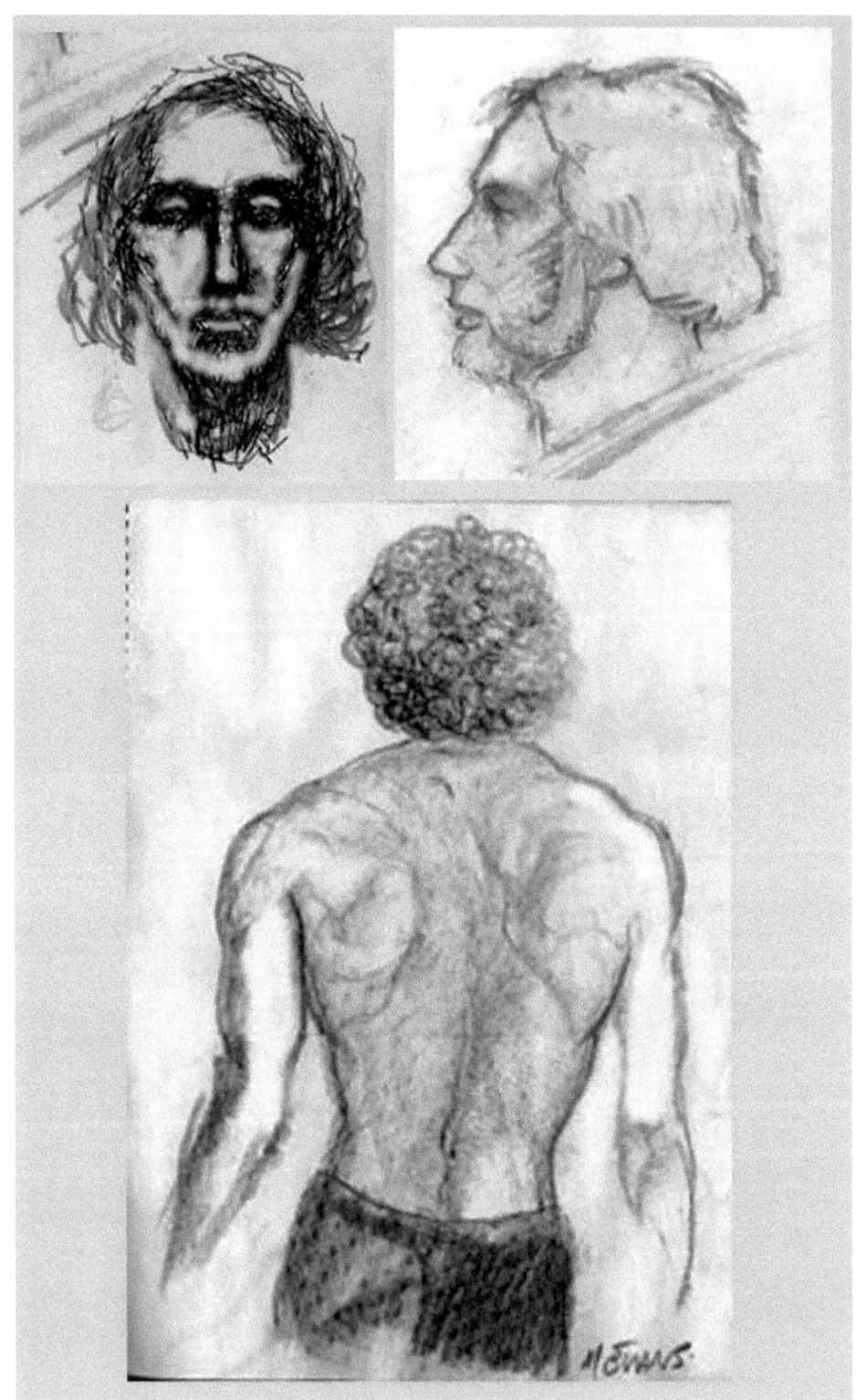

Primary Documents from 1974

Captions for various and sundry images from my sketch book:

Plate One: Bari Rolfe's class -- Masks were always a fun way of overcoming inhibitions; The "Neutral Mask" revealed your body's attitudes when you wore it; This curly-haired gentleman was one of our dorm mates; Joan Merwyn was from San Francisco, and already knew performers like Noel Parenti, Lorene Yarnell, Bobby Shields, and James Donlon; Joan's room mate Nancy also hailed from San Francisco. She possessed an radiant positive energy, inspiring all we others who came to learn. (Page 26)

Plate Two: Hovey Burgess and Judy Finelli were always teaching, indoors and out of doors. The constant juggling sessions attracted numbers of spectators at first, but everyone participated at last. (Page 27)

Plate Three: I could have behaved myself a lot better during the performance of fellow American Noel Parenti, but I laughed, and laughed hard, despite his unusual ideas and powerful technique. I knew Paul McCarthy, one of Conceptual Art's leading practitioners, but that was no excuse. Noel was a great tap dancer, and an even better man, who forgave me for my rudeness, accepting me as a friend. He enjoyed partying with us, and it was fabulous hearing stories from him, plus joining his physically excruciating early-morning warm-ups; Wonderful Carlo Mazzone-Clementi; James Donlon was a relatively progressive American, and an inspiration to our choreographer. (Page 28)

Plate Four: Stan (Jango) Edwards anchored an international amalgamation of talented performers called Friends Roadshow. Keyboardist Davy Norket led Friends Band. Few bass players could underpin his funky left hand, so they often toured without one. Young Justin Hammer was Jango's fearless partner in a variety of routines. Justin's mother Karen Harvey sang in Sail-Joia, a fine Amsterdam pop group; Roxanne Kelly sang the show-stopping *Taste Me* in the Friends revue; Rehearsing *Rockin' Robin* with Carl Holmer, Ted Van Zutphen, Mike Lynch, and Rick Parets. Backed by a Funk-oriented Jazz band, Friends Roadshow wove visual clowning, stand-up comedy, high and low art together in a colorful warp of theatrics. (Page 29)

Plate Five: Han Arai from Tokyo roomed with martial artist Shozo Sato. "We do a NEW Kabuki," he said proudly. David Carrillo signed on to the SLC Mime Troupe after serving in the US Navy. Hovey Burgess taught at NYU and at Ringling Brothers' training facility in Florida. Nancy returned to San Francisco, eventually becoming a leader in the amazing Burning Man movement and internationally renowned festival, which draws tens of thousands of artists annually. (Page 30)

Plate Six: George Kugler -- drawn while he was launching and catching Ping Pong balls with his mouth in the busy garden outside of the Viterbo College dormitories. With or without masks, Patsy Droubay always expressed her emotions very well in movement, and Carrillo partnered well with her onstage. (Page 31)

Absent Marcel Marceau owed much to Deburau, Barrault, and Charlie Chaplin for his famous silent character "Bip." *Children of Paradise* also featured Etienne DeCroux, Marceau's renowned teacher, as the blustery patriarch Anselme Deburau.

The crowd was very upset when it looked like Baptiste's big onstage break was interrupted. We raised a noisy un-mime-like fuss until the projectionist came down front and told us the film was simply cut that way. We later saw some other films which relied on action rather than words, but the most memorable to me was a black and white short called *The Factory* by Etienne DeCroux -- a hard-edged Modern Dance with masks in a checkered space. I could see that our dancers were already well-trained in an art form which matched and even exceeded many of DeCroux's artistic ideals.

A circus trainer from New York University named Hovey Burgess was on hand, along with his wife Judy Finelli. He carried duffel bags full of rings, sticks, and heavier balls with which he was able to teach the rudiments of juggling to dozens of people at a time.

One of the first sights I beheld from my dorm window was a statuesque dark-haired lady in the garden practicing the 'cascade' pattern. Her name was Nancy and she'd obviously had some training, plus knew how to teach. She regularly helped out neophytes like myself in the cool mornings before classes began. Before long, groups of people were everywhere on campus -- juggling some damn thing or combinations thereof. Hovey was often lurking around these clusters, passing clubs with Judy as his partner.

After less than a year of learning to be a theater technician, the idea of physically performing still felt strange. The aesthetic atmosphere was impossible to resist though, and I participated at first by doing the kind of art I had already trained to do. I'd left my video gear behind and since still photography was as new as theater to me, so I took out my sketch pad and went to work -- learning by drawing.

The very first class I attended as a sketching spectator was one of Burgess' basic workshops where he demonstrated how patterns of balls led to rings, and rings led to sticks, which led to clubs, and how two led to three, or two led to four, or five, and -- well he ended the demonstration juggling battle-axes while balancing on a stack of crossed steel cylinders. La Crosse balls, preferred by jugglers, were not available in La Crosse, but Hovey somehow bought his battle-axes there.

Later that week, we all took a trip *en masse* to Baraboo, Wisconsin, once the winter quarters for the Barnum & Bailey Circus. Dimitri was there, as were Czech expatriates Pavel and Citor. The circus graphics and memorabilia were fun to see, but the tired clowning under their big top was getting to be a drag until some young inmates from the Mime Festival started getting into the act. The cynical ol' carny in center ring even showed some life before we were done.

After a short time, it became clear that the hapless festival management was outnumbered and overwhelmed by the professional and carnal desires of more than a hundred men and women in their twenties. Across the street from the main theater was a place named the Wonder Bar, where beer sold for ten cents a glass. *Help Me Rhonda* and Chuck Berry's rather lewd full-length single of *Reelin' & Rockin'* dominated the jukebox. After dark, the REAL festival convened THERE.

The attendees quickly noticed that European acts outclassed the Americans every time, and that "Mime" was much more than aping Marceau's famous moves -- it was an ancient synonym for "Theater," with the same objectives. Strength, skill, surprise, and artistic insight were all-important keys to an audience's appreciation.

European artists like Citor Turba and Mummenschanz followed Dimitri's lead in shattering everybody's preconceptions, and lifting the proverbial bar of achievement high above the heads of even skillful Americans.

Everything we thought we knew about Mime was WRONG!

Bobby Shields was a strong, attractive American performer who was commercially successful at the time, but is now largely forgotten, or worse, sometimes being the target of ignorant unfair jokes because of his former fame. There were other shows by "establishment mimes" but they could trend towards the threadbare or even dull.

Hovey's teaching revealed the power, strength, and inspiration of traditional theatrical forms like Circus, and his Italian colleague, the great Commedia Dell' Arte master Carlo Mazzone-Clementi backed him up. When Jacques Lecoq arrived from Paris for his week-long workshop, it was official: *Everything You Thought You Knew About Mime Was WRONG!* -- an exhilarating and liberating concept at the farthest possible distance from disappointment.

Lecoq was a wellspring of practicality. Julie Taymor and Footsbarn Theatre studied with him in Paris, and his ideas formed the basis of future companies like Cirque de Soliel and the Blue Man Group.

Just when it seemed like things couldn't get crazier, Friends Roadshow drove in from Michigan with a small fleet of Ford trucks -- towing a portable stage, a funky electric band, a bevy of beautiful women, and long-haired men from all over Europe and America. They made everybody laugh with good songs, daffy comedy, and energetic physical performances. Friends featured talented female singers and a precocious lad named Justin Bishop-Hammer, Friends Roadshow's letterhead boasted companies in London, Paris, Amsterdam, and Detroit USA, plus Salvador Dali was their patron.

The Salt Lake Mime Troupe had already created a sensation or scandal, depending on who you asked, by taking over one of the performance spaces and putting on our own full-length show. I led the way in staging this coup, simply because I saw that Katie, Matt, Patsy, and Dave did work which was better than ninety percent of everything else presented at the Festival. Our performance was very well-received, but we made some waves nevertheless. When I spoke with Jango Edwards, the leader of Friends Roadshow, he suggested that we would do well in Europe, and he said could help us secure some venues there. He kept that promise within the year, but there was a lot more work ahead of us. In the meantime, we practiced our new-found skills all day and enjoyed being young all night during those warm and beautiful summer evenings.

Friends Roadshow played outdoors in Viterbo College's Rose Garden under the windows of the on-campus convent, but they also booked themselves into the same boogie joint on Main Street where I'd partied with Mamako. Friends also filled the Wonder Bar to overflowing with *de facto* block parties more than once.

Our pal George Kugler turned out to be an apt pupil when it came to clowning and juggling. He immediately innovated a wide range of tricks into an act all his own, along with a new character. He had observed the whole scene with a canny eye, and did us a great honor by asking to join us back in Salt Lake City. We accepted his offer, and never made a better decision. George committed himself totally to the art of entertainment for the rest of his life.

To top it all off, Nixon resigned during the last week of the festival, and we had the greatest celebration EVER outside in the garden of the dorm. Just before we drove off for Salt Lake, we watched W.C. Fields in a madcap juggling act on the TV. We stopped in Sioux Falls to visit with recently-graduated allies, saw Mount Rushmore in the fading blue evening, and made the dumb decision to drive all night but survived anyway.

Great Salt Lake Mime Troupe
Getting ready for The Road -- new members and the Glass Factory.

Many things happened in a very short period of time

Summary: The Mime Troupe played its first show out-of-state in Steamboat Springs, Colorado, and a few weeks afterwards was performing for a multi-level audience of peers and professionals at the International Mime Festival and Institute in La Crosse, Wisconsin during July of 1974. Nixon's resignation was a good omen. We were invited to perform in Amsterdam, Holland the following summer, but faced an awful lot of work to make it real. We were elated with new ideas and newly found confidence but were also dead broke and would need all of Providence's help in the days to come.

Almost the first thing most of us had to do when we returned to Salt Lake was find new places to live and work. Several among us also took trips to the West Coast -- Katie and David accepted an invitation from the Friends Roadshow to travel with them on a tour which ended up in San Francisco. Matthew Child and I went to Seattle, Washington and Davis, California. We visited Barbara Doherty in Seattle, Noel Parenti in San Francisco, and saw lovely Nancy at Project Artaud. We threw ourselves back into our work in Salt Lake because we all shared the goal of making Europe happen for us.

The Mime Troupe did some performances on television -- KUED (PBS), and several segments for KUTV, during which Matthew recorded an animated title for a regularly-scheduled local show, which increased our visibility. During the Autumn of 1974, the Mime Troupe performed at the Salt Lake Library at least twice; the Utah State Fair; the Hotel Utah; various venues around Arrow Press Square; the University of Utah at least a half dozen times; The Sun Tavern about twice a month; and several schools -- especially Oquirrh Elementary on Halloween. (Where Don Baxter, my sixth grade teacher, was Principal.) We were especially welcomed at Westminster College, repeatedly playing at the Student Union cafe, and teaching classes in Courage Theater, part of the historic main building with wonderful Dr. J.W. Lees.

George Kugler (Georgio) infused new positive energy into the Mime Troupe

Georgio worked on his juggling act before and after the movies at Trolley Square all week, and used his teaching experience to book himself in the schools. The greatest thing our La Crosse trip ever did for the Mime Troupe overall was bringing George into the group. I'll always remember the moment when he came up to me during one of our rehearsals and said "These guys are ready for center stage!"

I had the very same opinion, which was why I bucked the system to make sure the world saw what Katie, Patsy, Matt, and David had done -- plus hear the music by Paul, Stuart, Bud, and Fred. (We also had some angels on the festival staff helping us out.)

George had natural talent, and he saw how the Martha Graham-based training of our dancers powered something different from anything else America showed during the International Mime Festival. He also saw how he could contribute to our show and was inspired by our ambitions. It pained me to see him cheerfully hitch-hiking in the rain back to Seattle at the end of the festival because we had no room in our little two-vehicle caravan, but he showed up in Salt Lake City by mid August with his own VW bus, and outdid everybody in establishing our presence around the community.

We found a new studio right away

The Lollin Building, on Main Street in Salt Lake City. There were front and rear doors that we could use during business hours, plus a staircase from the alley. (Photo from the Utah Historical Society)

The Mime Troupe returned to Salt Lake and had to immediately vacate the Hillside Avenue building. Luckily, we found a space in Downtown Salt Lake City right above a music store where owner Gilbert E. Martinez generously let us bring all our equipment, create a rehearsal area, and start an actual business office. After I personally dug out a mountain of trash from the alley, we had access from the center of the block, up a steel staircase, or use of conventional doors on street level if we needed them.

We occupied the entire second floor. There were two long rooms overlooking Main Street -- I used the north room as my studio and it also doubled as our office. The music room was south of me, plus there was a small alcove with a telephone across from the cute little painting in the hall, leading to the dance studio which took up most of the middle and rear space. We never really got a chance to use (or clean) the third story.

People rarely looked up, but we watched a lot of urban living from our studio windows at the front of the Lollin Building on Salt Lake's Main Street. The Mime Troupe was ready to try new things, and we did -- most of our experiments were successful, although we failed once or twice. There were so many ideas ready to emerge from the ferment of the International Mime Festival. One of our best was a movement jam by Matthew, Katie, and George based on the concept *Competition*, which I verbally threw out for consideration at the start of a video session in the new studio. It worked beautifully, and I wish all our pieces could have been that easy to compose -- but they weren't.

Katie put in many hard hours working out movements. We did our best when we were preparing for actual shows, as Stuart noted -- luckily we had a lot of actual shows on our schedule. It wasn't always necessary to perform new material every time, but we needed to increase our repertoire for the sake of the audiences who repeatedly spent money to see us. The Sun Tavern was our most regular challenge. They were a jaded, er -- sophisticated, bunch who desired excitement and variety. We spent long nights in the studio preparing sets just for them, and they repaid us with appreciation and full houses.

Katie continued to teach at the Ballet Department, while creating new material for the Mime Troupe. Autumn was tough on Patsy, but she continued to hang in with us until we went on the road in December. Fred and Bud left after La Crosse. We not only needed to recruit new musicians, but Daniel Robert let us know that he was heading back to New York City -- luckily, he convinced the very capable Mark Nelson to be our manager. Mark was playing bass with my friend Sandy Duncan at the time, along with Curt Setzer, at The Pub in Trolley Square. Curt and Sandy would later form the Jordan River Uptown Band with Hardin Davis after we took Mark on the road with us.

Trolley Square enjoyed some early success with a complex of movie theaters. George performed his juggling act for audiences who were waiting between shows. He was competent, entertaining, and always innovating. The public exposure and good will were extremely valuable. George used his recent experience as a Kindergarten teacher to book workshops and performances in the local schools. We needed and appreciated his good-natured hustle.

As far as hiring our OWN musicians went, Stuart Curtis and Paul Blackwell knew a pianist named John Fischer. When John joined us, Curtis concentrated on his horns, but he was pleased to do it. Jan Fogel was a neighbor of Matthew Child. He heard her playing drums at a local night spot, and was impressed with her musical skill. She took a little convincing because her standards were very high. I was present when she first jammed with Stuart and Paul. Afterwards, I asked her what she thought, and she said "They have a lot of potential!" I ventured to say that a musician who could play bass and trombone would be ideal to complete the band. Very soon after that, I heard the band auditioning a person who could coincidentally do those very things, and when I asked Gregg Moore if he was going to work with us, he said "I sure hope so," and he did. Carrillo played congas and sang, plus Katie lent her capable voice to many arrangements. The Mime Troupe's band didn't acquire a name of its own until 1977, but it had a definite onstage identity, and was loaded with character and characters.

As we grew, the band played whole sets of music in various contexts. Besides Paul, Stuart, and John's original compositions for the dances, the current fashions from current bars and cabarets crept into our set lists like: Steely Dan's *Your Gold Teeth (See How They Roll)*; Stevie Wonder's *Sunshine of My Life* and *Superstition*; Marvin Gaye's *What's Going On*; and Buddy Miles' *Them Changes*. Katie sang a smouldering *Baby I Love You*, but I was also really happy to hear progressive Jazz -- like Miles Davis' *So What* and John Coltrane's *Mister P.C.*

Jango Edwards came all the way from Michigan to check out our work

We first met Stan Edwards when he brought the Friends Roadshow to the International Mime Festival and Institute. Everybody was stunned by their fleet of Ford trucks, the churning, powerful Funk band, the international cast, and their affable leader who called himself Jango -- commanding any crowd with a smile, wave, joke, or original song.

I was the first one of our group to meet them when they wandered into Viterbo College's gym to rehearse one perfect summer day. My sketchbook was at hand, so I got it out and made several pages of drawings as they came and went. (See the previous chapter for examples.) I'm sure he recognized kindred spirits when he met the rest of us in small clusters afterwards.

Jango repeatedly spoke of his desire to start another Friends Roadshow company in San Francisco, but it wasn't to be. I know he was seriously moved to see David and Katie in California as their transcontinental tour wore down in the aftermath of a gasoline crisis which made the economy of the USA completely different from the conditions Stanley Ted Edwards knew before he moved to Europe.

Jango had promised to book us in Amsterdam, so we were eager to show him what kind of show we were doing. Edwards flew out from Michigan to spend a week or so with us in November of 1974. Davey Norket arrived a few hours later, because of a mixup along the way. The Mime Troupe experienced another profound turning point that night in the studio above Main Street.

After we finally set up the instruments and rehearsal space for a run-through. Jango sat back at first to see what we did. He called a halt to things within minutes.

"You're used to professional audiences," he said, "I play professional audiences too, but entertainment itself is an art, and ANY audience will respond to entertainment!"

The rest of the night was spent learning Jango's songs which had served him so well in the Friends Roadshow -- they were simple, but contained dynamics which we had neglected in our own searching-around. I stood next to Davey and Jan as Norket arranged things on the fly, and adapted his rhythms in response to Fogel's amazing musicianship. Jango even made me sing too, so I could learn the same lessons our performers were learning about timing, pacing, and surprise.

We had several events scheduled for the two of them -- Jango would do a lecture-dem for Katie's Ballet Department class; The Sun opened their doors for us again; and the Art and Architecture Auditorium at the University of Utah hosted a formal concert for Jango and Davey. In between these things I drove the two of them to the first Kentucky Fried Chicken franchise on 39th South and State Street, and even took Davey to the sleazy old Jocor Lounge (pronounced Joker) for a much-needed beer. We left that bar and spent the afternoon at the University, where Davey practiced on the Bösendorfer grand piano at the Art & Architecture Auditorium while I gathered items we needed for Jango's "One Man Circus" performance a day or two later.

The Late Autumn weather in Salt Lake can be awesomely good, and we had absolutely beautiful nights and days. Even though he might have been a clown, Jango wasn't caught with his pants down at the Ballet Department -- his high-intensity workshop challenged even the most accomplished seniors, and we had a hard time following his skill and sureness over the next week. His impromptu lunchtime appearance outside of the Student Union wasn't forgotten for the rest of the year either.

I was videotaping Jango's performance at the University, so I couldn't do the lights. Luckily we didn't need much more than a follow-spot, and Carrillo's friend from Ohio, David Zupan, capably filled in for me. (He would soon take on a larger role in the Mime Troupe.) The concert itself was an amazing event -- they unlocked a Steinway piano for Davey instead of the Bösendorfer, but he wasn't bothered in the least to be playing another one of the finest musical instruments in the world.

Jango proved his contention that entertainment itself was fine art at the Fine Arts Museum -- his mixture of low and high comedy, plus verbal and visual acting, had people literally gasping for air. Carrillo assisted Edwards behind the fancy leather screen, and did a few small bits out front. A childhood friend of mine named Steve Blanc came up and said "That's REAL art!" at the intermission. It is too bad that nobody from the newspapers attended, even though we'd purchased ads -- Salt Lake City had never seen anything like Jango before.

Unless you'd been in that lucky crowd who filled The Sun to overflowing -- it was a magical night. The Mime Troupe's band lent Davy support, and our performers did a few pieces so Jango wouldn't have to carry the whole load. Edwards and Norket had no trouble at all -- they dominated the evening, and we learned an enormous amount.

By the time Stan and Davey were back to Michigan, we had two full sets of material ready to perform that we hadn't had before, and a new determination to give The Road a try. George Kugler took his van and rode over to the ski resorts of Colorado to see what he could find. Mark Nelson went to Southern California for the same reason, and we knuckled down for even more changes in our lives.

The group agreed on a subtle, but important, name-change

George came back from Colorado with TWO prospects for the Christmas season -- one of them, the Highlands of Aspen, confirmed their booking. We were very excited, but had to polish all our new material for the Glass Factory show first.

The reclaimed Glass Factory building contained a theater on an upper floor, with the quirky Dead Goat Saloon in its cellar. The audience there regularly patronized drama by the Human Ensemble Repertory Theatre -- artists gathered together from the community at large, but also including peers and some rivals.

As we were sorting out what we needed to do before traveling, we decided to rename the company one more time -- after the nearby lake rather than the town. It was a logical choice -- I'd had the idea myself earlier, and tacked up a whimsical logo-sketch over my drawing board, but I'm certain others had the same idea as well. Our two long weekends at the Glass Factory introduced the name Great Salt Lake Mime Troupe to everybody.

The Glass Factory's name inspired this image which also served us in a variety of gigs later.

Transcript of the review below from *The Salt Lake Tribune, Saturday, December 14, 1974* **And Music, Sound -- Mime Troupe Provides Entertainment at Glass Factory** by Irene Jones, Tribune Staff Writer

Mime is movement without sound, right? Wrong. At least according to the Salt Lake City Mime Troupe. (Sic: we were officially the Great Salt Mime Troupe.)

The mimists -- all 13 of them -- gathered at the Glass factory at Arrow Press Square Friday Night to present "Clown's Cabaret," a mime show complete with mime, music, and sound. The unusual presentation was comical, well-planned, nice to listen to and well-done. Find Seats   As the audience wanders into the theater to find seats, the mime/musicians are keeping early arrivers entertained with some fine jazz sounds. The mimists -- David, Matthew, Georgeo, Katie, and Patsy -- are seated around the room or wrapped around posts. Gradually the audience begins to realize that the show was under way and had been since the first person came into the theater. David and Matthew begin greeting the audience -- they shake hands, pat heads, remove shoes, scarves, hats. One girl is pulled from her seat and handed numerous invisible objects, which she graciously accepts. Finally she is allowed to return to the audience. The troupe mixes sound with mime, does some singing, gives us an intermission of jazz and a hilarious vaudville show for a finale.   Ping Pong Game   The sound comes during a ping pong game; foot races, a session where we learn what a shoe, hat, coat, and vegiweiner -- that's right -- is. Georgeo introduces the vaudeville acts with nonsensical descriptions, David manipulates a ventriloquist's dummy, portrayed by Matthew, the musicians leave their instruments and give us all a song and dance. And all of this is interspersed with mime. The mime is some of the best I've seen the troupe perform. Their puppet was flawless, moving each joint as the string was pulled. Expressions of hate, love, envy, disgust, pity, sincerity, mischief and loneliness were excellent. There was no story line to the show, merely a series of happenings that moved smoothly into one another. The Olympic medal winners suddenly were fighters; the fighters became arm wrestlers; they in turn, vied at ping pong; the ping pong game became a swimming meet -- or was it the other way around? The events were so swift and flowed together so well, the order of things becomes unimportant. Giving us relaxing jazz throughout the evening were Paul, Stewart, (sic) Greg, (sic) John, Jan. Mark, Mike and Dave -- the troupe is known only by first names. "Clown's Cabaret" will continue Saturday and Dec. 20 and 21 at the Glass Factory in Arrow Press Square.

Well, Mark wasn't making music in the show, and neither was Mike, but the reporter's enthusiasm was welcome indeed!

The Mime Troupe hit the stage at the Glass Factory uncharacteristically nervous and unsure. Van Hanson was doing the lights since I was swamped with other tasks, but that left me free to videotape the first night. They were FANTASTIC out there -- the best overall show since Steamboat Springs. I was smiling and relaying compliments to everyone afterwards, but they were depressed and unhappy -- convinced that we had failed. I immediately showed my overwrought company the replay, and their spirits rose to the heights they deserved to be.

There were a couple of mistakes, for sure, and a thing or two to correct, but the material was strong, and their performances had been superb. The Salt Lake Tribune's theater critic gave us a glowing review, which confirmed the video, and filled the Glass Factory for the rest of our run. Thanks to the Sony Porta-Pack, there would be no more bouts of stage insecurity within the group for a long time.

First Tour: Aspen Highlands
From a small city to the snows of an international resort.

Outta' State! -- More new faces and more new places to go

George Kugler invested his own money in a thirty-three foot school bus, which he then modified to as a mobile home so that we could go on tour with all our equipment, and every body would have a place to sleep, with storage for their personal items.

Carrillo and Zupan lent their skills to the project, and the bus was ready to go on the third week of December 1974, with Zupan as designated driver/mechanic. Mark Nelson assigned himself to follow in his own car, so that he could take care of business meetings and such. Twelve people set out for Aspen in the yellow bus-without-a-name as winter began in the Rocky Mountains.

Patsy stayed in Salt Lake to take care of her family, and we went on the road with Debra Ryals, a new lady recruited from the prolific University of Utah Dance Department. I am totally sure Katie and Jan appreciated her company -- there were loads of testosterone on that bus, and the women were outnumbered three to one by shaggy 70's type of men on their way to a new town for a very important gig.

We all knew that the Highlands of Aspen show was going to be a trial run for our planned tour of Southern California. Mark had set up a few appearances "down there" already. We had done our best "up here" to prepare the things we needed to succeed on the fabled ROAD, but nobody in our group had ever really worked in a sustained theatrical or musical tour before. We had so much learning ahead of us still ...

The Great Salt Lake Mime Troupe hits THE ROAD!

Our venue was a relatively new development at the base of the mountains west of the main town of Aspen. The view from the hotel/resort faced east towards Aspen Grove and Eastwood. It was warm and sunny when we arrived, but it tended to snow at night, and daily temperatures were about to DROP as Christmas and New Year approached. Nelson had already scheduled some shows in Southern California and met us in Aspen.

After an all-day drive from Salt Lake, we parked the bus at the Highlands resort as night was falling. When we went inside we found out: We were expected, but the size of our full company and five-piece band hadn't sunk in with the management team; The building of the stage had barely started, and there were no plans made about where we would sleep; The manager who booked us was away and wasn't expected back for a few days. Luckily, the staff on hand found rooms for us, and we scrambled the whole next day to get the material and tools needed to finish turning the dining room into a serviceable theater.

Instant Theater -- Just Add Sweat!

The main hotel dining room where we played had a cathedral ceiling reaching three stories or more up to the steep peaked roof. We took over the far east end. The view in back of our newly-built stage was snow white and sky blue or black both day and night. We had to figure out how to compete with God's own visual handiwork somehow.

Foremost among our allies was "Fast Eddie" the chef -- he and the other workers at the Highlands gave us immeasurable assistance throughout our stay, and we couldn't have succeeded without them. Ken White's portable lighting system was flexile enough to light the stage and band, plus there were some additional effects available by way of the existing decorative lighting. George, Carrillo, and Zupan doubled the size of the stage and tore out some barriers. By the time we had our premiere, the dining room only gave up two tables, and we had enough room to perform along the east end, with the band spread out along the whole wall. There was a tiny changing area at the right where the dancers could enter and exit, but we made do with minimal costume changes, plus the performers gradually grew comfortable with entering and exiting from any direction. I worked the lights from the audience in a front corner at the right.

We signed up to play three shows a day: Things worked out so that *apres ski* featured the band at about 3:30 PM -- their smooth soulful arrangements of familiar songs went over very well with both young and old listeners winding down from their days on the slopes; Late nights became a showcase for short comedy pieces, like we used for street theater, plus Jazz and Pop Music, as well as Jango's handy material from the thick Friends Roadshow book of swipes.

Depending on the day of the week, night sets could be short to extensive. One evening, during a long "party night," the young couple near me mentioned "we have a group like that back home." It turned out that they were from Michigan, and knew the Friends' songs, so we had a fun conversation about Stan Edwards, Senior Class President at Milan High School, before he thought of calling himself Jango; At 8 PM we unleashed *Clown's Cabaret*, straight from the Glass Factory -- our well-rehearsed combination of raw entertainment and high art was totally unexpected by the vacationers on hand, and they ate it up, as well as doing the same with Eddie's excellent dinners. They also told their friends and acquaintances.

Aspen had a reputation for being a playground for the rich and famous. Some of our customers may have been fortunate in their lives, but we spent almost all of our time around people who worked for a living. There was gossip that Diana Ross was vacationing in Aspen. She was a major movie and music star at the time. One person swore they saw her "smiling at our street show," but none of us ever saw her, or anybody from her entourage either. I didn't doubt that Ms. Ross was around, but she was likely more interested in winter sports or private affairs of her own. Whomever spread that rumor gave our performers some severe cases of nerves over the unlikely and unfulfilled possibility of Ross seeing us -- a social game which really puzzled me.

What drew wealthy visitors to Aspen was the abundant snow, which generally fell every night, with sunny days following. The elevation was slightly over ten thousand feet so the snow was deep and powdery over a substantial base. There were great views, good accommodations, and easy access to the Denver airport.

The only celebrity any of us met was a very pleasant man named Ed Ames. He and his brothers had a successful singing group in the 50's, and he'd been a TV actor too. His all-too-accurate hatchet throw on the Johnny Carson Show was rerun every holiday season for over twenty years. Mr. Ames was staying at The Highlands and stopped by to see what we were doing late one night. The band had just played a round of music, and Georgio the Clown introduced the Siamese Twins -- Matt and Carrillo came onstage with their heads sticking out of one big overcoat. There was some absurd banter, and the act ended with Debra and Katie joining in, draped in another greatcoat as the Twins' wives. They danced offstage to many gruffaws and shaking heads. Ames left discreetly, wearing an inscrutable look on his face, but everyone else was laughing!

Two overcoats plus four dancers gave us the surprisingly fun "Siamese Twins" number. We created this act to lighten up a Sun Tavern show which was getting too serious, used it successfully in many street performances and developed further variations for a couple of years.

Work, work, more work -- is there time to play and sleep?

Besides all the hard work, we had time to play. The Highlands had an outdoor heated pool at the end of a tunnel running from the sauna, shielded by hills and steam. Bathing suits were optional after 10 PM, but simple civil behavior was common and customary.

It was the holiday season, and space was at a literal premium in and around Aspen. I'll never know why the manager and his brothers never thought about our accommodations ahead of time, but we were sluffed around to several locations, including a bunk house, humorously named "Rick's Racks" during our engagement. Carrillo didn't think it was very funny, and stayed in the bus a couple of times out of pique ("I've BEEN in the Navy!"), but it was about ten degrees below zero, and he couldn't run the motor all night. He had enough bags and bedding available to get by, but his idea didn't work for the rest of us in that ultra-cold climate.

We all were leaning about what we needed to have on hand for work, and for living, and how to keep track of them in transit. Quarters far from the venue without personal transportation required a new kind of discipline for everybody.

Getting the word out on the streets

Ready, Aim, Fire! *The nearest thing to a dragon ever seen on Aspen's streets is this fire breathing member of the Salt Lake City Mime Troupe who wandered through last week. The Troupe, which mixes classic mime with theater, vaudeville, sideshow, and music, will be performing at the Aspen Leaf restaurant at the Highlands through New Year's Eve with a show guaranteed to amaze, delight, and entertain.* Photo by Chris Cassette, from the Aspen Flyer December 31, 1974

When we got into town, we found that we had a lot of advertising to do, because our venue was outside familiar local paths. Except for George, the Mime Troupe was unfamiliar with the dynamics of street theater at the time, but it was necessary to be seen by the public, and show them something which would convince them to come and watch us perform. The company did some short skits, and reworked some of Jango's silliness in between George's sharp juggling routines, honed on the bricks of Trolley Square. Downtown Aspen was an odd mix of hustle and inactivity, depending on the times of day and degrees of coldness. The company and I did publicity for our out-of-the-way venue. By just trying to stay warm during promotional street performances, Katie began to develop a character named *Madame Zablouva* from under her scarves.

The band did their best, but the freezing temperatures and noisy environment presented challenges which weren't resolved all at once. My part was to circle the crowds and hand out little fliers telling about The Highlands, and our show. I also hung posters where the businesses allowed it. Georgio finally got his unicycle rolling under his feet during our Aspen trip.. We met a wonderful comic actor named Jean Paul Bell for the first time, and renewed our friendship later in Amsterdam. We had to be back at the hotel before 3 PM and spent most of our first week making our rounds midday as the temperature got cold, colder, and INTENSELY colder.

On one intensely cold day, I heard someone calling my name down by Mill Avenue while finishing my duties. I turned around, and saw Eddie and his girlfriend waving at me. They lived nearby, and asked me to come along and visit. I gladly accepted -- calling Mark to let him know where to pick me up, once I got inside.

The first thing that impressed me, besides their generous hospitality, was a Salvador Dali original on the wall. We warmed up and just talked for a little while. Eddie had to get back to work in another couple of hours, but we had time to play a few vinyl records on his excellent stereo. He owned a brand-new album by Phoebe Snow, who would be a star in a few months. I asked if they liked hearing rich, deep bass, and put on the Beach Boys' *Holland* album, cueing Dennis Wilson's moody *Steamboat*. The tune was mellow, but the bass shook their townhouse all the way to the roof. Eddie laughed in surprise and said: "I hear you're supposed to be going to Holland ..." I nodded my head and told them both about Steamboat Springs the previous summer, also expressing my hope that the coincidences concerning this tasteful album were good omens for our ambitions.

Once it was looking like our promotions were paying off, the hotel offered us access to some ski passes and rental equipment. I was a pretty inept skier, and adverse to any more freezing. So given a choice, I skipped the group's first (and last) cross-country expedition. The people who already knew how to ski did alright, but it was a struggle for the others. Afterward, one or two troupers took to the slopes at times, but most of us stayed indoors. Our drummer suffered a bad fall on the cross-country skis, so the doctor put a splint on her right wrist. Jan would play with her left hand for most of the next two months -- keeping her right hand suspended, and using her feet liberally. The music that came out of her kit was still in perfect time, with excellent flourishes and bright percussive touches. She was a jewel on the throne.

Our manager Mark had his car with him, and ferried us between the local radio stations, and business offices. He showed us a tiny dulcimer, less than a foot long, which he was learning to play. He was developing a repertory of Folk songs, and it was fun to sing along, and puzzle out the beautiful little *Epinette des Vosges*. He would later become an acknowledged dulcimer master, and record several albums using this family of instruments.

The New Year -- with a new chapter on the horizon

We did our job well by filling the Highlands' restaurant/theatre at all hours with customers, as word of mouth spread around the ski slopes while New Year Weekend approached. I'm not sure what we would have done without Jango's material from Friends Roadshow to back us up as the night sets got longer and longer. *Clown's Cabaret*, with all that Modern Dance, was still the most popular and admired thing we did, though, and it was booked solid for most of a week at the end of our run. I was very pleased to see many couples and families returning more than once, and bringing guests with them. "We're here to see YOU!" they told me repeatedly, and we always exchanged thanks.

New Years Eve was a long haul for the band -- the party went late, and there was a lot to do the next day, including packing up all the clothes and equipment onto the bus for a long drive back to Salt Lake City. The trial run was over, and trial though it was, we acquitted the appeal of our performers and material before a world-class audience. We had one last meal together midday at Eddie's house before we rolled out of town. He made sure we all had as much of his superb cooking as we could stomach, and filled our containers. He sincerely wished us luck on our upcoming California tour, and was certain we would do well in Europe.

Road angels like Fast Eddie were our greatest blessings as we traveled. There were some hard lessons to be learned from our experience, too -- We made jokes at the managers' expense from the start, but they got the most lucrative laugh at the finish, when we had to pay a substantial bar bill.

The bus would become well set up for sleeping later -- but we made do with the vehicle as it was while Zupan, George, and Stuart took turns driving in the gathering gloom towards Utah. Sometime during the night somebody woke me up with the lights fully on and another party starting. Eddie's packages were quickly unwrapped in celebration of our first tour as a group. The hard work was over, and it was really time for some human bonding. We laughed about everything that had happened, and finally turned in for a few chilly hours near Price, Utah, since nobody wanted to drive anymore. Dawn broke, and it only took a few hours to make it home to a town which wouldn't be home for much longer.

California: Part One
THE ROAD winds on to San Diego.

Snow to sunshine -- touring in Southern California

Summary: The Great Salt Lake Mime Troupe tested its new material at The Highlands near Aspen, Colorado with amazing success, despite a handful of problems. The bus needed a little more work so that everyone could stretch out and sleep, but Carrillo, Zupan, and George were up to the task.

When we got back to Salt Lake City, the Sun Tavern asked us to perform there for its regular clientele once again before we left for San Diego, the first city on our tour of the West Coast. I borrowed some lighting equipment from Van Hanson of the Human Ensemble, and took it back before we left. The Sun helped us put a sharp edge on our show and we were grateful to them. I packed up the next day, which was almost as dark as the previous night in Utah's smoggy winter, and sipped one last beer at the corner disco across from the railroad depot before starting my trip to sunny California.

We also bought a Melodica for John Fischer from Dave Faggioli's roommate, and cleaned out the Main Street studio. Everyone had to find storage for their possessions with friends and family, because we would all be gone for quite awhile. Debra stayed in Salt Lake to dance for Patsy's senior presentation, but rejoined us in March.

Most of the group left ahead of Mark and myself once the bus was ready. Mark drove his own car -- he and I switched drivers as the other slept. We didn't have all that much in common before the Mime Troupe, but through several conversations we discovered that we had both worked with a dancer named Francis during the RDT Video Workshop in 1973 -- I had supplied Ravi Shankar's *Sound of the Sitar* album, and an LP with Stockhausen's *Kontra Punkte*. Mark mixed the two together at the campus radio station for a strong solo dance by Francis, who was surrounded by video feedback generated by her movements and the music. It was the best piece that came out of the workshop, and we were both proud to have been part of such a fine project.

Jimmie Rogers sang: *I'm going to California, where they sleep out every night!*

We stayed east of the main city of San Diego, in the hills of La Mesa. Katie's brother was our host, and we used his connections as a teacher to help us find much-needed rehearsal space in a junior high nearby, we also used his hot water liberally. Our sleeping bags were spread-out between the bus and the house. Rituals and patterns of meals and rest evolved during touring.

Debra had stayed in Salt Lake, so Katie and Jan were the only women on the bus. I'm not saying we guys were a totally insensitive bunch of idiots, but I'm not claiming the opposite either.

Mark had booked Southwestern College and San Diego State. School shows started right away, thanks to George, but we needed more work! We got rehearsal space at a nearby junior high for most evenings, and an increasing list of school shows.

Southwestern College was located in the little town of Chula Vista, in sight of the border between Mexico and the United States. They liked old movies -- a 16mm copy of *Singing In The Rain* was circulating around the classes in the Theater Department. We didn't run up walls like Donald O'Connor, or hoof around in puddles like Gene Kelly, but I figured that the iconic Marilyn Monroe would help attract this particular crowd, so I modified our Sun Tavern poster with her face redrawn in stark black-and-white from Norman Mailer's best-selling biography, and it WORKED. It was fun to make "Warhol Walls" by multiplying the image in certain locations on-campus, but we needed the posters elsewhere, and I could only indulge myself to a limited degree. After this concert, we retired Marilyn because I wanted to advertise our uniqueness and originality, but the two occasions we recruited her were a lot of fun!

The campus boasted a number of new buildings, including the massive white edifice which was the home of their theater. I've forgotten the professor's name, but he acted like a gruff east-coaster on the outside, yet possessed a heart of solid gold. "Some of these Mime people we get here are really lousy!" he said with a level, challenging gaze.

I was still wrung out by the long journey from Utah, but looked right back into his eyes and told him "Our company will do things you've never seen on a stage before," with an easy confidence which I never lost during all the years I spent with the Mime Troupe. I had variations of that conversation many times, and gave the same assurances with no reason to regret them afterwards.

Our first tech rehearsal in that big theater was a new challenge to me, but the calm technician in charge made everything comprehensible, if not easy (it wasn't). When the dancers finally took to the air after a long wait, the professor smiled, and kept smiling whenever we were around.

The Southwestern College concert's greatest importance was that it was our FIRST performance in California. It was roughly divided into two halves -- 'serious' pieces at first and Clown's Cabaret after the intermission. The first part wasn't all THAT serious, and we also transitioned into some highly-charged Modern Dance during the second half.

After we hit our climax, and the audience was profoundly hushed, George introduced David Zupan as our fire eater. He was broad-shouldered, short, but muscular, and was assisted by tall, thin David Carrillo on the huge dimly-lit stage while the band played suspenseful music. After a couple of big blowtorch-like plumes of flame, he tried a trick which Jango had suggested back in November -- Carrillo brought out a bowl of lamp oil with a flaming coat of lighter fluid riding on top. The upper level burned at a lower temperature, so the effect was stunning when Zupan sipped from the flaming vessel and spit out another huge arc of dragon-breath.

I had spent hours arranging permission for this segment. Katie's mom was in the audience, and thought that it was something we didn't need, after we respectfully asked her opinion. As it was, Zupan's final stunt resulted in some of the lighter fluid entering his lungs. He gradually developed a serious pulmonary inflammation which laid him up in the hospital and could have killed him. On occasion, Carrillo continued fire-spitting for us, with a bit more subtlety, but nobody tried the lighter fluid trick again. Momma was correct and we gradually retired that whole sideshow act.

Sundays in Balboa Park -- Street Theater outside the Botanical Gardens.

Simultaneously with rehearsing for previously-booked shows, and lining up schools, we were also on the lookout for new places to play. Street theater had previously worked well for George, but the extreme cold in Aspen discouraged the rest of group to various degrees. When we heard that Balboa Park allowed open-air performances outside the Botanical Gardens, we grasped at the opportunity anyway, and it turned out to be a fabulous way of spending Sunday afternoons. The park had rules, but our band had everything they needed to make fabulous music outdoors and still be legal. We earned some spending money, made contacts for new jobs, and met some wonderful people.

One person who sought us out in the park was local star Don McLeod, AKA *The Modern Mime* -- he had previously led a progressive rock group called the Mime & Music Machine, which toured with barnstorming acts like the early Fleetwood Mac and Deep Purple. He was very supportive of what we did, and continues to make a career using his considerable physical skills long after we've drifted in different directions.

We all learned to "Do Street" by repetition and practice. My job was to made sure we had flyers of upcoming gigs, and to hand them out to interested parties. If someone spoke about hiring us, I'd direct them to George or Mark. We played half-hour sets, with half-hour breaks outside of the Shade House. During down times, I wandered around and juggled on my own, drumming up customers for the next show with a touch of white makeup on my face, wearing generic 'civilian' clothes instead of a costume.

We worked the enthusiastic crowds of weekend visitors. The dancers learned a vast amount about comic timing with short routines -- punctuated by George's rapidly-improving announcing, and shamelessly stolen jokes. The band's music was solidly entertaining, and they even clowned around a little. Jango's wacked-out routines came in handy. We also made a point of driving the bus down to the Pacific Ocean and enjoying the fabulously warm weather which lasted all through January.

One of the finest people we met at Balboa Park was a young San Diego State University student named Karen. She was performing as a solo clown, and asked if she could shake my hand. When I gave my consent, she took my wrist and gently rocked it back and forth, my hand shaking in response. OK -- at least I thought that joke was funny. By the end of the day, she invited the whole Mime Troupe to stay at her house.

We parked our bus outside and she cleared space for those who wanted to sleep inside. It was exceedingly kind of Karen to treat us like Robbie had treated his sister's friends when we weren't even relatives. We troupers stayed with her several times during our sojourn in San Diego. It impossible to overstate how much we owed to Road Angels like Karen, who generously helped us out along our adventuresome way.

San Diego State University -- Concerts at the "Back Door"

Mark Nelson booked us for a couple of weeks at a small concert hall called the Back Door, downstairs from the busy Aztec Center at the center of the campus. It was a long, somewhat narrow place with a raised stage at the far right corner. Unfortunately it was too small for the dancers and the band, so we set up our musicians on the floor in the other corner. They had a small, but reasonably-powered PA system, and we borrowed a channel to set a microphone on Jan's drum kit, after noticing from the booth how she was muffled by the stage and amplifiers. There was a moment at the beginning of one of our sets where the dancers would leap from the stage and visually introduce the band as they kicked the tempo of the music higher, and Stuart launched a soaring sax solo.

Most of the places we worked in during the mid-70's needed two people to operate the lights in an average theater -- one in back, switching the lights, and pushing rheostat faders up and down, according to cues given by another person with a view of the stage, namely me. In contrast, the Back Door's lighting was wired to a console in the sound/light booth on the other side of the hall with clear sightlines on the show.

The stage manager was a student employee named -- something. I have obviously forgotten his name, but he was known as Lord Lumen, and I've never forgotten THAT. He was enrolled in the Modern Dance Department at SDS, and I learned a lot about operating solid state thyristor-controlled systems from him.

A View from our Audience of the Great Salt Lake Mime Troupe:

Daily Aztec San Diego State University Tuesday, January 28, 1975
Stage Review by Randy Schultz

As the audience begins to filter in, a fine six-member band sets a relaxing mood with light jazz. Then, ever so gradually, two or three mime artists begin to interact with the audience. After a while you realize that the show you've been waiting to see has already started.

The nine performers of the Salt Lake City Mime Troupe (sic), which should be named the Salt Lake City Circus, quickly overwhelmed audiences last week at the Backdoor with an amazing combination of traditional mime, vaudvillian comedy routines, juggling, clowning, song, dance and music. And every bit of it was superb.

The opening set consisted of traditional mime -- some of the best I've ever seen. The mime artists -- Matthew, Katie, George, and David (the troupe is known professionally by their first names only) -- run through scenes depicting an indoor track meet, a boxing match in which the microphone goes down for the count, and Olympic medal winners who suddenly become fighters, then arm wrestlers, and then ping-pong opponents.

But the order of the scenes is unimportant. They change so swiftly and fit together so well that it is hard to tell where one ends and the next begins.

Not only is their mime hilarious, but also very moving. In portraying the classic emotions of love, hate, sympathy, pity, and loneliness they also take a piece of your heart.

The highlight of their mime set occurs in the "Puppet" segment. David finds a puppet, played expertly by Matthew, and humorously manipulates his strings, pretending that the puppet is his friend. In a sensitive and moving scene David gives Matthew his own heart so that he, too, may live.

After an intermission and some less traditional mime, the band steals the show for a while. Consisting of Paul on guitar; Greg (sic) on bass, trombone and tuba; Jan playing one-handed drums (she had a cast on her right wrist, but still outplayed many drummers); John on keyboards and trumpet, and Stewart (sic) on sax, flute and clarinet; they play everything from hardcore blues to jazz to hardcore rock and roll -- and play it to perfection. In fact, they're laced so tightly together it's amazing they can still breathe.

Now if this isn't enough Katie sings like Lydia Pense (of Cold Blood) and David can charm an audience as well as the Kinks' Ray Davis, the result: everyone in the place was on their feet dancing and having a good time. The Salt Lake City Mime Troupe's good vibes are totally contagious.

But the show's still not over. After a short break comes the circus set, where George as M.C., introduces a number of freak shows and outrageously funny acts. The band members make fun of Hare Krishnas, Matthew portrays a man who talks backwards, and Katie, Matthew, and David are the Marvels in a great spoof of 40s song and dance. George, portraying Georgeo the clown, highlights this segment of the show, however, with his tricks and coy, silent humor. Especially entertaining is his juggling of a grape, an apple, and ahead of cabbage, while simultaneously eating the apple.

After more than three hours of solid entertainment, George apologetically announces the end of the show. The nine performing members of the troupe, all accomplished artists and professionals, have enjoyed the show as much as the audience. But exhaustion takes over, and they reluctantly head back to their "house" -- a converted school bus. Nobody likes to see a show this incredible come to an end.

You probably think it sounds like the Salt Lake City Mime Troupe's performance was one of the best live shows I've ever seen. And you're absolutely right.

Mr. Schultz was very perceptive. His compliments were welcome, and we used them in our publicity for a long, long time, but he touched on a couple of observations which were more profound than he might have known. The members of the troupe DID enjoy the show as much as the audience, but exhaustion was becoming a problem, and could literally "take over" when we least desired it. The bus was suitable for sleeping -- barely, but most of the seats had been removed to make it so, and travel could be tiring, especially if we went north to Santa Barbara and back in one weekend. In retrospect, we were starting to "live for the show," while deferring some important personal issues, which would arise anyhow.

Dare to compare -- Alwin Nikolai Dance Company at San Diego State.

We got a break on tickets, and I watched the concert with Frank Sanguinetti's daughter from Salt Lake. So who's Sanguinetti? He was director of the Museum of Art at the University of Utah, and we haunted the same hallways in the Art and Architecture Building. I even took some Art History classes from him. His daughter recognized my face from the Art Department, and Alwin Nikolai's company brought us together to see their performance, a long way from our home towns.

Nikolai's company was metaphorically Major League, but our choreography, music, and theatrics would leverage our own group into Triple-A. The Mime Troupe joked afterwards about dancing in sleeping bags, referring to the abstract costumes we'd seen on-stage, but it was a good experience to see how far Modern Dance had come in bringing lighting, movement, and music together. We were thinking of ways we could out-do the masters once we got the chance.

Grossmont College, shows and more shows, and the Bus gets its own name.

One Sunday at Balboa Park a couple of young people who were members of the student government at Grossmont College saw the Mime Troupe performing. They spoke to Mark and George, and we set up a *de facto* partnership where the Mime Troupe did a series of free lunchtime performances at the Student Union advertising a full concert on the weekend, where we would then sell tickets and earn some much-needed money. The student government built a big raised stage. The splintery plywood floor drew some uncharacteristic complaints out of poor Katie, though. We recruited a man from their theater department to flip switches in a blind closet while I used whispered cues and hand gestures during the show -- responding to the action based on the music, and shadows on the back wall. We frankly wondered if our gamble would pay off, but the concert was a winner -- Carrillo sat Matthew the Marionette on his knee and greeted *Gross-em-out College* to wild laughter from the audience.

Sometime during our engagement at San Diego State University, Matthew Child declared that the bus needed a name: "How about something like Hobart?" If it was so moved, seconded, and passed without any objections or real parliamentary procedure at all.

The reader may ask: "Why Hobart?" I say: "Who knows?" However -- there was a Hobart Street in San Diego, just off El Cajon Boulevard, near the SDS campus, and if my memory serves me well, we often drove down that very street on our way to Karen's bungalow. I once asked Matthew while we were in Southern California if that was our connection with the name of our bus, but after a moment he just shrugged.

California Tour: Part Two

Rainy Season on THE ROAD in Santa Barbara.

Hobart the Bus heads north on wet Highway 101 for Santa Barbara County

Summary: The Great Salt Lake Mime Troupe played in Balboa Park every Sunday, many school shows, a private party or two, at least one bar, plus some recreation halls while touring around San Diego. We also performed concerts at three colleges that rewarded us with full houses and a glowing review. Road Angels Robbie and Karen let us share their homes. Mark Nelson had gone ahead of the company to Santa Barbara and Zupan was with him, after leaving the hospital. People told us that the Mime Troupe could actually base themselves in San Diego if we stuck around, but there were other bookings further up the coast. Once we left, the sunny weather turned rainy.

Once again, our company was totally unknown to the community when we arrived, and we had to start the process of unpaid street shows and footpadding for publicity all over again. The Santa Barbara Museum of Art allowed us to put on street performances at the foot of their stairs. City College of Santa Barbera hosted several outdoor shows, which brought many people to the theater. Mark had arranged performance space at the Santa Barbara Playhouse, but we were also sharing the place with a local children's theater production. Luckily the experienced staff were able to juggle our mutual needs, in different ways, and I learned some additional skills which would come in handy very soon.

The Santa Barbara Playhouse was an elegant building which was totally demolished for a commercial development over time. It was set back from the street at 124 West Carrillo. The front was classic California Deco, with a dash or two of Spanish detailing. The reception area was shallow and wide, but comfortable. They had a big airy backstage area and a wide stage thrusting deep into the audience, with a curved front apron just above the eyes of our front row viewers.

Seating in the auditorium was broken up in various ways -- there was a side gallery, close-in chairs set along the arc of the stage, and an upper gallery which wasn't uncomfortably high at all. I recall a lot of railings though. The lighting booth was comfortable, with a great view of the whole house. One day there was an electrical problem at the children's show, and I was solemnly told they had unplugged my lights. I just laughed -- I only used a few specials for the dances, and left the other company's set-up intact. We were back to normal in 3 minutes.

We first stayed outside of the main city near the University of California at Santa Barbara, in a colorful suburb of the town of Goleta called Isla Vista. A very nice lady named Joanna was our contact with the local Arts Scene, and she found some opportunities for us to perform street shows and conduct some classes.

Our 'workhorse' poster for Santa Barbara et cetera -- I had drawn it for Aspen, but we didn't start printing it until Southern California. This is an early draft, since the final version featured liberal sprinklings of musical notes among the juggling balls.

Although it was fun, Goleta turned out to be a bit too self-contained for our needs, since we needed customers in the theater we were renting -- an inconvenient distance away. We could put up posters in the small commercial center of the Isla Vista, but they were torn down if we posted any on the University campus, since we weren't sponsored by any formal organization there.

We traveled back and forth to Santa Barbara in order to perform at the City College, which was a wonderful place to gather enthusiastic crowds -- the views of the beach were fantastic, the students there lived close to the Playhouse, and actually came to our shows! When we played our first concert, those City College students were there, but our audience was otherwise sparse. We needed to do even more work fill the seats, which was getting harder to do when we weren't getting paid to do it.

We knocked on every door, and revisited every venue that allowed us to play. We did at least one bad street show out of exhaustion too -- not for the first or last time. There were other frustrations: I crafted a series of colorful banners which I had to take down again because they broke local signage rules; George convinced one of the local newspapers to send a reviewer, but the guy was a petulant jerk who wrote about lights being in his eyes -- which they weren't. There were these kinds of things and others, but I'm remembering too many negatives -- our efforts paid off in community-wide good will, and soon-to-be full houses, so we didn't go totally broke. We also won a glowing review in another newspaper.

The best example of Santa Barbara's good spirit was Road Angel Margaret, who invited us to park the bus at her sprawling house right in Santa Barbara. She was a tall, dark-haired lady with a wide circle of friends. She loved Nina Simone, and I did too. Our band included the Jazz standard *St. Thomas* in their set after hearing recordings from the actual island of St. Thomas at Margaret's house. One of her many friends was a Latin bandleader named Pinche Pete. We met so many nice and helpful people just by going to see him. One of them sponsored a private engagement at the Playhouse after we completed our formal run there.

Concerts by the Great Salt Lake Mime Troupe utilized transitions from character-driven comedy to poignant touch-and-go relationships as a prologue to our dances. Katie and Matthew acted out conflict, and then danced it, The pair worked out one soaring dance piece over a Jazz composition featuring Stuart and the band playing at a frantic tempo in 5/4 time.

The dancers took to the air, and audiences gasped when Katie and Matthew swung their limbs in counterpoint and unison while suspended in the air. They repeated the movement until the crowd, at least, was out of breath,. As the dancers' feet struck the floor, they vividly expressed their emotions as they glided towards and away from each other. The action went right to the ground towards the end, as their conflicts created a carousel of circular attraction and repulsion. *Five Four* never got a real name besides its time signature, but everybody who saw it remembered the small, intense duo flinging themselves back and forth, forward and back, and up and down onstage.

The grace of Matthew and Katie brought tears to many eyes as this duel of dance technique and raw emotion unfolded before the stunned audiences. They flew like birds during Dance sequences. These moments of concentrated energy and purpose brought in many repeat customers and impressed the critics. The two dancers kept the competing energy going in a much sillier number afterwards, which brought the audience back to primordial clowning and white-faced buffoonery, but before they settled down they uncorked another masterful Modern Dance and sent everyone to new heights again.

Yet another audience view of the Great Salt Lake Mime Troupe:

Santa Barbara News and Review February 14, 1975
Theater by Elizabeth Sutherland

The Great Salt Lake Mime Troupe, now performing at the Santa Barbara Playhouse, is without question one of the most purely entertaining and talented young theatre companies I've seen anywhere.

It is exciting to see performers possessed of such an abundance of vitality: not only are they energetic, they are both individually and collectively unique. The group consists of 14 members, including the mimes, a fine ensemble of jazz musicians, and three supportive members (the manager, stage and lighting technician, and a fire eater). Although the group originates out of Salt Lake, they now call their yellow school bus home. By traveling through various states, they hope to secure the exposure and publicity which will lead to financial and artistic recognition. From my perceptions and the response of the audience, they should not have any difficulties reaching their goals.

The show began with some extraordinary sounds from the musicians, who remained situated on stage during the performance. I found myself becoming so absorbed with the music that I almost forgot there was more to come. The musicians, who met at the Westminster School of Jazz in Utah, helped to bring about a fine mixture of music and theatre. The actors came together at the University of Utah School of Modern Dance, and they are brilliant.

Katie, Matthew, David and George combined dance, mime, vaudeville and circus acts to increase the awareness and perceptive pleasures of each member of the audience. Their exaggerated facial expressions and crisp fluent body movements are the essential -- each member exhibits attributes of a successful mime; totally distinct personality and sensitivity. Katie, I felt, was particularly fascinating.

Groups like this one need our support, and the best support we can give them at this point is to purchase a ticket for their show. They will have three final performances at the Santa Barbara Playhouse on Feb. 13, 14, and 15. While in town they are also giving demonstrations and teaching classes at UCSB. Tickets are on sale at the Playhouse at 124 W. Carrillo, 966-1061.

Cussing and discussing -- A short break before Los Angeles

I have avoided writing about our conflicts in the Great Salt Lake Mime Troupe, but anyone who knows about human nature can guess we experienced them, and they'd be correct. We had a serious discussion overlooking a beach to the west of Santa Barbara about what the group would do next. Los Angeles was on the agenda, but there weren't many bookings right then. "It's a big city, and it's just going to SUCK!" was one canny observation,

L.A.'s importance as a center of entertainment was pointed out by several others, and the goal of Europe reinforced the positive side of that debate. We agreed to split our forces -- Mark, George, David Carrillo, and Michael (me) would work on preparations in Los Angeles while the rest of the Troupe drove Hobart the Bus back to Salt Lake for ten days. We would then re-convene in L.A. to see what kind of recognition we could achieve, and hopefully attract the attention of an agent to find us some more reliable work. David, George, and Mark drove down to the city, and I took a Gray Line passenger bus to meet my hosts there.

California: Part Three

THE ROAD runs on forever and Los Angeles never seemed to run out of ROAD.

EL-LAY: Swimming Pools, Movie Stars -- and itinerant artists on a bus

   Summary: The Great Salt Lake Mime Troupe spent the first half of February 1975 in Santa Barbara, California. Looking ahead, we agreed to split our forces -- four of us would work on preparations in Los Angeles while the rest of the Troupe drove Hobart the Bus back to Salt Lake for about ten days. (We would re-convene in L.A.) Carrillo, George, and Mark drove down to the city, and I took a Grey Line Bus to meet my hosts in Pasadena.
   Once I settled in as a guest of Paul & Karen McCarthy and Al Payne, Mark Nelson then found ME, and we got to work setting up our initial gigs, and trying to find new ones -- paid and unpaid. Al drove me out to his workplace at California State University in Allhambra. Mark and I also visited UCLA, sadly without success, but the City of Los Angeles permitted us to do street shows in some prestigious public venues.
   Nelson had contacts at the University of Southern California who set up a performance where we shared the receipts. Student Activities arranged this joint venture like Grossmont College had done -- there were posters to draw, print, and post, plus the hall needed preparation for dressing rooms and lights. I composed and inked the USC poster while listening to the album *Burning* by a group from Jamaica called the Wailers. Mark and I also stuffed envelopes at the Century City Playhouse with manager Ivan, while the Kinks sang about "Motorway Living" over the P.A. I painted a banner for the marquee at Paul's house -- luckily he had the room to allow me to work this way!
   We desperately needed some kind of a place to park Hobart the Bus when the rest of the group arrived. After a lot of searching, I was present when Mark's future wife recalled a friend named Martin, who worked at a junior high school and owned a ranch house in a canyon near Tajunga, in the northeast part of the L.A. area. Their friend generously opened his house to us, and arranged rehearsal space at his school too. Road Angel Martin's place was a welcome relief from LA's hustling insanity. Katie first sang *Sitting Here In Limbo* while rehearsing at the junior high where he worked. As we were getting ready for one of our first shows in Griffith Park, we got our call confirming that we were booked at the Festival of Fools in The Netherlands!
   The Century City Playhouse was a small theater, restricted to 99 seats by local rules which were too complicated to discuss here. Weekends were devoted to another play sponsored by Actor's Equity and we had to share the space again, like Santa Barbara. We coated a large flat with black photography paper and masked off the entire stage behind us. I used some different colored gels, and a few specials again, but left the other group's lights untouched. Dressing rooms were no problem. Loading in and out was easy, and the lighting booth was efficient.

The show MUST go on -- So the show DOES go on

Recognize THIS? We used Clown's Cabaret as our public theme again and played in Century City at a 99-seat venue managed by a delightful group of exiles who began their own All-L.A. saga in Santa Monica as an alternative theater ensemble.

The remainder of the company arrived in Los Angeles after a rather hectic trip to Salt Lake City. Katie had been honored for her courage at the Dance Department, but there were mostly domestic tasks on everybody's agenda. Besides Hobart the Bus bringing the Mime Troupe, Zupan delivered my Volkswagen to me so that I could take care of my stage management tasks without interfering with Mark's mad scrambles around the city. David Carrillo and George had borrowed occasional motorcycles from friends, so we needed the extra vehicle very much. Martin's Tajunga hideaway was a godsend, but we also stayed at Katie's parents' house, and with her sister. The Appenzeller Clan were amazingly gracious Road Angels throughout our Southern California tour, and Katie's childhood friend Barbara became both a Road Angel and fellow-traveler.

Patsy was still taking care of her family in Salt Lake City while the Great Salt Lake Mime Troupe was touring in Southern California. Debra had done very good work for us in Aspen, but she had commitments to meet when we got back to Utah. Jan was the only woman in the band, and Katie was our only woman dancer when we were gigging in San Diego and Santa Barbara, although Debra visited us a few times. Matthew had been one of the best male dancers at the University of Utah, and partnered with Katie very well. Carrillo performed whole sets with the band, singing, playing, announcing, and other 'front man' duties. To say that we missed Patsy and Debra is an understatement.

Patsy had not let her responsibilities stop her creativity, however, and she choreographed a dance that featured Debra Ryals in a duet with lean, lanky stained glass artist Paul Fisher who we knew from Hillside Avenue. The video-tape of their piece cheered us up greatly in Los Angeles, as did the great news that Debra would be rejoining us for our Pico Boulevard engagement.

Antonin Hodek and I finally saw each other again, six long months after we met at the International Mime Festival. When I first arrived in Los Angeles by motor coach, Road Angel Karen generously rearranged her schedule to drive me around the maze of freeways, since she was on spring break from San Diego State University. Her family lived towards the north, so we had lunch, and I tried to pay back the infinite debts we owed by introducing her to some of the few contacts I knew in the area.

Hodek was first on my list. He made friends with me immediately when I arrived at the International Mime Festival the previous summer. Karen and Tony got along fine, and stayed in touch for awhile. Hodek laughed about the Mime Troupe's plans for Europe, since he'd spent so much time and effort relocating to the United States.

There was an active "Mime Scene" in the Los Angeles area, as one would expect. Teacher/performer/stuntman Richmond Shepard called himself "America's Foremost Mime," and gave us personal encouragement. He organized a Los Angeles Mime Festival later that same year, which included Joan Merwyn (our masked friend from La Crosse) but we were far away by then.

One More View of the Great Salt Lake Mime Troupe from the Audience:
Los Angeles Times (1975) Stage Beat by Lawrence Christon

Kinetic Mimetics at the Burbage

The Great Salt Lake Mime Troupe at the Burbage Theater is a group of gifted young performers out of Utah consisting of four mime players and a jazz quintet. Purists may deride their liberal use of music and occasional narrative, but unlike several other mime troupes hereabouts, their approach is rooted in the dance, which affords them exceptional command of their bodies.

As they are mostly in their early 20s, their material may be described as a mimetic counterpart to what was a while back known as Stoned Humor. Their routines transform themselves quickly and with eloquent and spontaneous ease, and are performed quite innovatively. They're a little ragged in spots (particularly in a lame ending to their Clown's Cabaret segment which inadvisably brings some shuffly musicians into the act), but chalk that up to immaturity. They have the rare virtue of being hip.

If they can hang together (they're traveling as a collective so idealistic that they eschew names) they will be extraordinary. 10508 W. Pico Blvd., Century City, 839-3322. Tuesdays through Thursdays, 8:30 p.m. until March 13.

Matthew and Carrillo in "Puppet" inspired two captions: The LA Times said: MIME EXPOSURE Members of the hip and eloquent Great Salt Lake Mime Troupe; The Santa Barbara News and Review wrote: The Salt Lake City Mime Troupe is living out of a school bus, touring the Southwest and hoping "to make a lot of friends."

While Mr. Christon was attending our performance, he sought me out in the booth at intermission, and was smiling! He said our show was "very unique," and asked about our background. I told Mr. Christon how we met at the University of Utah Dance Department. His review in the L.A. Times immediately brought in some much-needed business. We had been doing shows at various schools around the area too, and there were more of them being booked every day.

On the scene in 70's Los Angeles -- peers and allies

There is much to say about what was going on in the rest of the town while we were trying to make our mark. A couple of women who had toured with the Friends Roadshow were doing stand-up comedy in small clubs as the Lady Friends. They were very sweet, remembering us from La Crosse, and the Friends Roadshow's ill-fated trip to San Francisco. Ivan arranged for the Mime Troupe to see Lady Friends perform in Beverly Hills at a nightclub called The Daisy. Besides us, there weren't too many customers on hand. They sang a beautiful song with taped accompaniment mixed by Carlos Munoz, keyboardist for the Beach Boys at the time.

The only contemporary celebrity we ever saw on our California tour happened to be at The Daisy that night -- Jim Brown, the great NFL running back turned action-movie star, but his table didn't seem to too impressed. Ivan and Leonard, the even-tempered managers of the Burbage Theatre Ensemble, made many things possible, even outside the doors of the playhouse. The reason we even in The Daisy at all was because of Ivan's colleagues known collectively as the Mystic Knights of the Oingo-Boingo. They worked various odd jobs, and helped the Burbage Theatre Ensemble with printing posters and distributing them around the vast L.A. area. They also performed regularly in Beverly Hills, winning an enthusiastic audience with their high-energy shows.

There were almost a dozen performers, featuring guitars and horns, and broad theatrical stunts like playing Duke Ellington songs from the 20's in gorilla suits, and constant blackouts with scenery and costume changes. One of their co-leaders came down to the Playhouse to see our show and even sat in with our band. We did the same with other musicians and singers, but Danny Elfman would later turn Oingo Boingo into a successful Rock act, and take his own career even higher by writing some of the best and most popular movie soundtracks of the late 20th Century.

Marcel Marceau and Claude Kipnis did concerts while we were touring the place. (Matthew saw Marceau -- good show!) Jack Albee cleared the way for our group to perform outside the Los Angeles County Museum of Art. There was no money in it, but the exposure was invaluable. We were in good company -- Bobby Shields was there a few years before us, and Robin Williams would be there a few years later.

James Donlon had been one of our inspirations and mentors since Daniel Robert sent the dancers in the Mime Troupe to Brigham Young University to see the Menagerie Mime Theatre -- a San Francisco ensemble of four young men who worked visual magic onstage with their flowing movement. When we saw Menagerie again at the International Mime Festival in La Crosse, Wisconsin, only Bob Francesconi and Donlon performed, but they were stars of the American contingent, including Bobby Shields and Noel Parenti -- who were also based in the San Francisco Bay Area at the time. Shields' wife and partner Lorene Yarnell stuck around La Crosse to take advantage of the learning opportunities at the festival, while Bobby went elsewhere. The very physically imposing Shields did teach an informal acrobatic workshop before he left, demonstrating methods of falling without injuries.

Donlon was on hand throughout the festival, and taught classes for people of varying backgrounds and abilities. He took time out to preview and critique the Mime Troupe's concert. Katie especially valued his opinions, which were quite positive in La Crosse. We somehow got in touch with Donlon, and he came to see us once more at the Century City Playhouse. He was audibly displeased by Jango Edwards' influence on our material, and although he praised certain individual details of the concert, the overall shape and direction of our work was NOT to his liking.

Donlon also spoke of performing in places which presented an artist in the best possible setting, and arranged for us to see his one man show at a college in San Fernando Valley. It was divided into two sections, like our show, with the initial set consisting of short scenarios. The second part was entitled *We Are All Clowns*, where Donlon incorporated lessons learned from Swiss clown Dimitri, Czech expatriate Citor Turba, and other Europeans. The very pleasant theatrical scholar Bari Rolfe, co-director of the International Mime Festival, was in the house, and we had another La Crosse reunion.

It was an exhausting period of time. We tried taking trips to the beach, or going to Ojai Canyon, but the daily grind of driving long distances on the freeways for mere survival money was taking its toll on all of us. We enjoyed a few good times at the Century City Playhouse, and awe-inspiring moments in front of young students, but we also suffered some too-empty houses, and bad shows at critical times, when we just couldn't overcome our exhaustion.

The lows seemed to overwhelm the highs when they happened, despite the gains we had made in the tough City of Angels. When a specific theatrical agent declined to represent us, it frustrated Mark's main goal in coming to Los Angeles. The group voted to forego an additional week at the Century City Playhouse in favor of doing school shows, sometimes three a day, for the rest of our California sojourn.

Our final farewell to the motorways of Southern California

We made a few appearances at Loyola-Marymount University near the beaches because of a young filmmaker who contacted us in San Diego, followed us to Los Angeles, and asked our performers to act in a film for him in whiteface.

On one of our final mornings before returning to Salt Lake, we were getting ready for an early morning street show on the Loyola-Marymount campus when the fuel cable broke on our bus, less than a mile from our destination. It could have been worse, but it was still bad -- about a fourteen inches of cable hung in the engine compartment, with about six inches to go before it could reach the throttle. George and Zupan worked out a scheme where the former sat next to the engine, working the carburetor while the latter signaled with the gas pedal.

I drove my VW close behind Hobart the Bus as we moved slowly in rush hour traffic. A police car smoothly cut in front of me at the first left. We were all praying aloud that they wouldn't see George, but as we stopped at a sign, the rear door flew open and there was Georgio the Clown, partially costumed, with a very concerned expression on his half made-up face when he spied the cops -- who immediately made a deft right turn and quickly drove away. We did several street shows at Loyola-Marymount University, shot footage for a film unseen by any of us, and played our last formal concert in Los Angeles on their campus.

Our wintery welcome back in the Rocky Mountains

I lent the VW to Matthew Child so he and some of the other Troupers could take care of their personal business further up the West Coast. Mark Nelson drove his car in the convoy with Hobart the Bus as we wended our way back to Salt Lake City in order to get ready for our transcontinental journey to Friends Farm in Milan, Michigan, and the Festival of Fools in Amsterdam, Holland.

Sunny green California springtime turned to overcast brown winter in the high deserts of Nevada and Utah. As we climbed towards 4000 feet we started driving through rain, which turned into snow on our second night out of L.A. While Zupan steered the bus in near-whiteout conditions, I kept my eye on the right edge of the road .

As we hit the pass above Payson, Utah the storm ceased, and we saw the Wasatch Mountains stretching out northward under a moon which was just past full -- lighting the entire way to Salt Lake, several hours further on in the post-midnight cold.

There would be more hard work ahead of us -- Hobart needed refurbishing, and our show needed adjustments for Europe, but the Great Salt Lake Mime Troupe had been tested in the crucible of the Real World, and was ready for whatever came next.
That is, after we ALL got some rest!

Coast To Coast To Europe

THE ROAD runs through Utah, Colorado, Kansas, Michigan, New York, and onto Capitol Airways.

Passports and another concert at the University of Utah

Summary: The Great Salt Lake Mime Troupe attracted favorable attention in Los Angeles at the tiny Century City Playhouse, earning a laudatory review in the *L.A. Times*. The daily grind of driving long distances on the freeways for mere survival money took its toll on all of us, though. Amsterdam's Festival of Fools had confirmed our booking, and we pointed the bus eastward to continue our coast to coast drive.

The Great Salt Lake Mime Troupe in Spring 1975: Clockwise from upper left --Paul Blackwell, Matthew Child, John Fischer, Katie Appenzellar, Stuart Curtis, Georgio Kugler, Gregg Moore, Jan Fogel, Debra Ryals, David Carrillo, and Patsy Droubay. Photo courtesy of Stuart Curtis

The Great Salt Mime Troupe had a lot of toil ahead of us in order to be ready for a tour of Europe. We rested for a few days after returning from Los Angeles, and then began our tasks. Hobart the Bus had sprung a leak or three, and water seeped in. George, Carrillo, and Zupan changed all the foam rubber and carpeting, after caulking the seams. I tuned up my red Volkswagen and put it into the hands of Carrillo, who drove off to do the chore of organizing our upcoming tour from Friends Farm -- Jango's base near Detroit, Michigan. Many company members had already given up their apartments, and stayed in Patsy's home overlooking the city. Matthew took our passport pictures there. We got our paperwork together, plus packed the myriad items we needed on the journey ahead.

Spring at the Art & Architecture Building

We might have felt pretty weary and isolated at times, as we learned what THE ROAD really meant, but we convinced many people along the way that we were the 'real thing' and they came through for us when we needed them the most. Mark Nelson's allies in ASUU Programs sponsored a concert for us, and Bruce Fugit from the Dance Department furnished all the lighting equipment we needed. My friend Lennox Tierney waived the auditorium fee, and we put on a very good show, despite an experiment or two that we left out later. We couldn't call it a benefit concert, although it was, but my last Mime Troupe poster in Salt Lake City honored the many 'angels' who helped us as we made our way in the world.

Challenges abounded -- we noticed that our performances were getting faster from familiarity and we needed to readjust the act so that we were neither rushing nor padding things. Patsy rejoined our group, and Debra was still dancing for us -- along with the joy of their participation came responsibility to create material which matched their talent. Which meant that Katie, our busiest performer, had even more to do as a choreographer -- without rehearsal space, or even a home address. Tension was mounting!

The Great Salt Lake Mime Troupe was still gathering members -- Road Angel Barbara McCarthy came out from California to do what she could. George fell in love with a woman named Chéri and asked if she could accompany him. What could we say? George had been our greatest single benefactor, and a truer friend would have been impossible to find. He still had his VW van, so their privacy was no issue, and we had learned the value of having another vehicle in the convoy besides unwieldy Hobart.

So in April 1975, two years after the Mime Troupe began in the concrete halls of the Art Department at the University of Utah, we left Salt Lake City on a journey to the other side of the Atlantic Ocean. After wintery Wyoming, our first stop was Denver, Colorado, where we lingered for about a week as guests in a large house with a huge yard in the suburbs, thanks to relations of John Fischer. The Mime Troupe did some workshops at a local school where John's sister taught classes. It was warm, and we enjoyed our stay, but we didn't play any real shows during our time there, although George was looking really hard for opportunities. Cultural highlights I remember were Star Trek reruns, Linda Ronstadt's big breakout album *Heart Like A Wheel*, and trivial, but outspoken, disagreements about the quality of the very popular J. Geils Band.

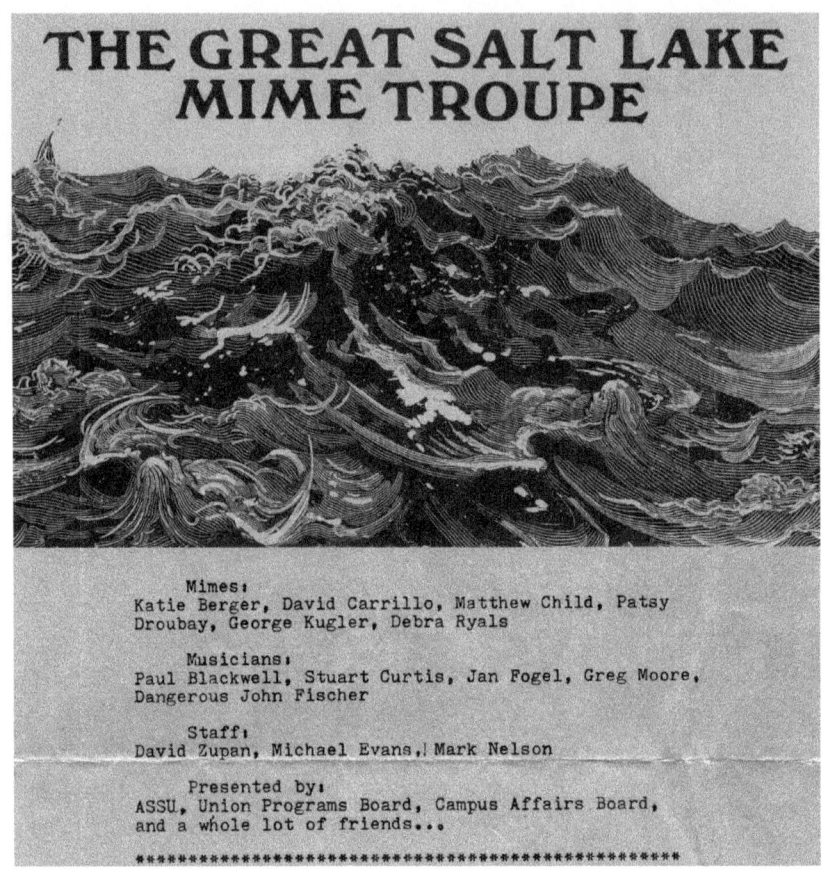

Details from the program for our Special Concert (Prior to European Tour) in the Art and Architecture Auditorium at the University of Utah during Spring 1975. The poster featured seagoing angels by Gustave Doré in honor of the people who helped us on THE ROAD.

Goodbye and Hello to Winter -- Trekking across the Great Plains

Europe still beckoned --- One sunny morning we packed up and headed east on Interstate 75 towards Kansas, Missouri, and St. Louis, where we needed to pick up a Trouper's birth certificate. Eastern Colorado is (in) famous for heavy snowstorms in the spring which can be well over a foot deep. Midday, the sky turned gray, and a swirling snowstorm surrounded us. A raging wind blew steadily from the north. Our windshield wipers were running at full speed, but we could barely see well enough to drive.

I was one of two spotters at the front, helping the driver keep eyes on the edge of the road, the traffic ahead of us, and George and Chéri in the VW van. We knew better than to stop. Our gas tanks were full, and there were abandoned vehicles here and there to remind us what would happen if we didn't keep moving. It was still daylight when we crossed into Kansas with the storm behind us. Hobart was encrusted with snow on the whole north side -- all the way up to my elbow in places as I knocked it off. The south side was only wet with predictable slush and road-dirt.

Our heroic *Quest for the Missing Birth Certificate* took us through Kansas City, and onward to St. Louis. I drove George's VW Bus that night, and saw dawn breaking over farms and back roads as we found our address out in the fields of Eastern Missouri. We were all legal to travel to Europe, but had to make one more overnight trip through Illinois and Indiana before approaching Friends Farm, near Milan (pronounced MY-lun) between Ann Arbor and Detroit, Michigan.

Dining with Friends, sleeping with Friends, and every other thing -- with Friends

Friends Farm had been the headquarters of the American Friends Roadshow for more than a year. There was a freeway entrance nearby, and the rural area was peaceful, but not isolated at all. A big central farmhouse anchored the property and several outbuildings added to the available housing. Jango also rented space to a couple of mobile homes on the property. We never met these renters, and could only guess what they thought about the constant comings and goings. We parked Hobart The Bus in their driveway, and made the place our home for a couple of weeks.

The very first thing after our arrival was a jam session -- Joe Lovano and another man showed up who had formerly been in a European combo called *Bumbalee!* They were gigging in nearby Detroit, liked to play Wayne Shorter tunes, and enjoyed exploring Funky Fusion Jazz. We unloaded instruments and amps, then our musicians started playing for hours on end.

I just thought the whole thing was totally COOL, Although I was very tired, I spoke with Jane Hunt, who was sitting next to me. We remembered each other from La Crosse the previous summer. Jane was a singer with a big bluesy voice, originally from Los Angeles. Most of Friends' other woman singers had left, and she bent my ear about days when dozens of Americans and Europeans flocked to Jango's home turf in Michigan, then faced an oil crisis which drained the economy.

Among the pictures I remember seeing on the walls was a photo of sax legend Boots Randolph, the brash full-color Friends Roadshow poster by Matt Rideout (see page 72) hanging near an understated black and white composition, resembling a playing card, with former Friends co-star Nola Rae wearing a clown nose -- a delightful red dot in the center of the duo-coloured print. I was also impressed by a signed Picasso hanging discreetly in the living room.

In 2010 Stuart Curtis described making music at Friends Farm:

I was very glad to meet and hang out with Sean Bergin at the farm. He was and is a very passionate and worldly player and took it upon himself to mentor me. I was very green around the gills he helped me find my way as a player through the next several years. Sean is still a fixture in the Amsterdam music scene.

While we were there, Joe Lovano stayed at the farm for a night or two while he was playing at a jazz club in Detroit. I think Sean had gone to hear him and invited him back to the farm to stay. He was a relative unknown at the time, but since then he has come to be a major tenor saxophone player in the jazz scene of the last 20 years to the present.

The mime troupe band was rehearsing, and he sat in. We played Dizzy Gillespie's "A Night in Tunisia", and he took a solo over multiple choruses that left us all astounded by his technique, ideas and musicianship. The rhythm section finally ground to a halt as everyone stopped playing but him. He just kept boppin' away. We were simply awestruck.

The Friends were mostly Americans up front -- Jane Hunt sang, Carl Holmer did stunts and sang, Rick Parets was an ace stand-up comedian who sang too. Michael Novotny was an imposing comic actor with great presence, who often acted as MC when Jango Edwards wasn't running the show. Michael sang a gut-busting version of Carl Douglas' *Kung Fu Fighting*, a major hit at the time.

Helena Van Danzig was an ex-ballet dancer from England who had been in the London Friends. She could do anything onstage with an easy grace, and was *de facto* manager of the company. Sean's English-born wife Janine ran the homestead at Friends Farm -- their little daughter was named Thembi, after an album and song of the same name by Pharaoh Sanders. The band consisted of Davey Norket, Ced Curtis, and Sean Bergin.

A Diversion: Friends Roadshow's album collection

There was a small, but tasteful collection of records at Friends Farm. Among them were The Pair Extraordinaire, a funky combination of a singer with string bass accompaniment; Cream was long-disbanded, but far from forgotten; Grover Washington Jr. was just starting to climb the heights of popular Jazz/Funk.

Heigh Ho! Heigh Ho! It's back to work we go!

Jango made arrangements with a Detroit bar named The Filling Station, one of the venues on his circuit, to introduce our act to Michigan over a weekend when Friends was traveling elsewhere. The Mime Troupe was pretty nervous about the whole thing, but we needed the work and experience. One disturbing fact was that we couldn't fall back on Friends' tried-and-tested bar material, since the upcoming crowd had seen it already. George led the way as MC of *Clown's Cabaret*, and we did our goofiest Mime Troupe scenarios. We had a few rough spots during the first night, and the owner sat us all down to say "You're not the Friends Roadshow!"

We deserved better than that, and knew it -- the next night was remarkable for its high energy and confidence. Fundamentally, we didn't change things much, but used this occasion to try out more characters, and different costumes. The owner even congratulated us, as if he thought he had something to do with it -- well maybe he did, if standing up to him counted for something. Friendly Joe Levano came by late one night to encourage us. On one of those nights in downtown Detroit, perhaps the second, we suffered a malfunction in the electro-mechanical system of Hobart The Bus. We couldn't go any faster than about fifteen miles an hour. At first we thought of bedding down, parked on the street until morning, but we changed our collective minds in an hour, although we were never threatened or anything.

We limped all the way to Milan in the far right lane of the freeway by the early morning light, and Zupan totally rewired Hobart The Bus' engine in Pontiac, Michigan a bit later. Back at Friends Farm, we scrambled to pack what we needed for our upcoming tour of Europe. Our preliminary itinerary had not only Amsterdam, but the Hot Theater in The Hague before the Festival of Fools even started. After that event, we had an opportunity to tour rural Southwest England with Footsbarn Theatre -- they had traveled to Tabarka, Tunisia with Friends Roadshow, and Michael "Madness" Novotny was a founding member of the company.

Try as we might, we only had two more gigs in the USA ahead of us -- an outdoor appearance at the University of Michigan, and an actual theatrical concert at a high school in Jackson, Michigan, arranged by Stuart Curtis' family. We visited the famous Blind Pig tavern in Ann Arbor, but never played or jammed in that space. John Fischer DID sit down at the piano, though, and noodled around a little. "There's sure been a lot of blues played in B-Flat on this thing," he said.

In between the delightful jam sessions at Friends Farm, we watched late night rock concerts on TV to keep up with the times. Besides the influential Ohio Players, we were impressed by the awesome lead vocals of The Stylistics, and classy presentation of The Natural Four (*I Got Work To Do*). Curtis Mayfield was always excellent, but we noticed how the producers spliced footage of people rubbing their eyes, children sleeping, and even a Bassett Hound yawning as it got later and later. We also enjoyed the boneheaded horror flick *Willard* -- rats and all!

I personally practiced my own juggling tricks outside, behind the house under a large tree, spent a lot of time in Novotny's studio making graphics, plus threw darts in the music room with thoughts of English pubs running through my mind. There was ONE special afternoon where Friends Roadshow and Great Salt Lake Mime Troupe spent a rare day-off together, playing football (soccer), drinking beer, and sharing food.

Another Diversion: More Road Albums -- on the radio and off the radio

Hobart the Bus wasn't wired for stereo. AM Radio had to serve us as we drove from place to place. One or two musicians had cassette tape players, but we heard most of our recorded music on the road as guests at people's houses -- either from FM Radio, or vinyl long-playing records. The three albums discussed below are just a tiny fraction of what we heard.

Johnny Winter And (The McCoys) introduced *Rock N' Roll Hootchie Koo* on their first album, but songwriter Rick Derringer also sang a version of Steve Winwood's lament from the road -- *No Time To Live*: **I've given everything that was mine to give, And now I turn around and find that there's no time to live.**

Jackson Browne's *Late For The Sky* featured a Magritte-inspired cover with lettering by psychedelic poster artist Rick Griffin, and a sensitive violin by guitarist David Lindley, Two songs hit a chord of familiarity for me -- one was called *For A Dancer*: **Into a dancer you have grown, from a seed somebody else has thrown. Go ahead and throw some seeds of your own ...**

Browne still performs *Before The Deluge,* his paean to youthful idealism in his live shows: **Some of them were dreamers, some of them were fools ... As their hands reached for the golden ring, with their hearts they turned to each other's hearts -- for refuge ...**

Tom Rush was popular when I was in high school, but the public had largely forgotten him by the 70's. One afternoon I spied a copy of *The Circle Game* -- with songs by contemporary stars Jackson Browne and Joni Mitchell, who were "unknowns" when it was originally produced. Hearing the first recorded versions of those fabulous tunes was a pleasure for every listener: **And they tell him, take your time, it won't be long now -- 'till you drag your feet to slow those circles down!**

Are we ready for Europe yet?

The Mime Troupe parked Hobart at Laura and Charles Curtis' house when we were in Jackson. These particular Road Angels treated us fabulously -- Laura Curtis helped arrange our performance at Jackson High School as well. Laura was part of the Jackson Area Dance Council, and had arranged for the Alvin Ailey Company to appear there too. Her daughter Martha Curtis was a first-rate modern dancer.

Our final two performances before take-off were diametric opposites. Jackson, Michigan was the kind of venue that we did best -- a dance concert with new and old material, featuring a magnificent creation by Katie which utilized all of our trained dancers in circular motions which took them high and low around the stage, accompanied by a lushly-arranged rondo written by John Fischer, which swirled and tumbled like cascading falls in a river. Our audience was attentive, quiet, and deeply appreciative of all they experienced.

Patsy and Katie renewed their collaboration on their first trip to Holland, and continued dancing in America and Europe until the late 1970's.
(Photo by Jan Jaap Dekker)

The long-arranged showcase at the Ann Arbor theater festival was an anxious event, even before we arrived. Matthew had spent much of the night awake at Friends Farm, printing photos for our press kits. The concept of "showcase" meant that we were supposed to impress promoters and agents, but the organizers were extremely vague about who would be there to see us -- communications between them and "fringe performers" like Friends Roadshow and ourselves became even more vague as the date approached.

Our show was good -- George, Carrillo, and the band performed with particularly high energy and skill in an outdoor brick courtyard with a small crowd present, who searched their programs in vain for us. Good thing a banner with our name was overhead!
All but one or two of the festival staff were indoors, as were most of the journalists, promoters, directors, producers, and agents who were supposed to see us. The one write up I saw about this festival dismissed all its outdoor performers in a single sentence. I'll never know if Helena actually did the topless fire-eating routine which Jango planned for Friends Roadshow or didn't bother -- but the solitary critic never mentioned anything like that!

The lettering brush and myself

During our layover in Denver, Colorado, I got orders from David Carrillo to paint a large banner, which would be used at an outdoor appearance at the University of Michigan in Ann Arbor. It was basically good news that we were booked in a theater festival at such a prestigious venue, but kind of bad news for me -- I had made one successful banner for the group in Los Angeles, and one total failure in Aspen. Both of them had taken a great deal of labor, and the process of making those kinds of things was the kind of commercial art I'd never enjoyed.

While developing the banner, I also crafted this logo, used later in the 1970's.

Fortunately, I had time to research this project, so after buying a proper brush at the University of Denver one day, and looking through the bookstore for a manual which could teach me something, I saw that Dover Books, the great publisher of public domain material, had reprinted Helm Wotzkow's *Art of Hand Lettering* in a durable paperback edition which fit my meager budget perfectly after spending twenty-five dollars for the brush. (Which I still own.) There was no way of practicing on the bus, but I hit my lessons hard when we arrived in Michigan. I chose "swash capitals" for our banner, and painted the 10 foot by 4 foot monster on the stage in Jackson, where we later performed our last full concert in America that year.

As we embarked for Europe, the Great Salt Lake Mime Troup consisted of six dancers/performers and five musicians: Paul Blackwell, Matthew Child, John Fischer, Katie Appenzeller ('Duck'), Stuart Curtis, George Kugler, Gregg Moore, Jan Fogel, Patsy Droubay, David Carrillo, Debra Ryals -- plus five support people: Barbara McCarthy, David Zupan, Chéri Burke, Michael Evans, and Mark Nelson.

Michigan, Ohio, Pennsylvania, New Jersey, Manhattan, and Queens.

On the night of our departure, I parked my Volkswagen at Road Angels Laura and Charles' house in Jackson, and took Amtrak to the train depot, where Hobart The Bus picked me up for the final drive to New York City and JFK Airport. I can remember observing the lit-up house of Friends Farm from the freeway, and wondering if I'd ever see it again. (No, it was sold in 1976.)

There isn't much I can tell about our headlong dash to the Atlantic Coast -- I slept during the day, and kept the driver alert at night. I recall a few flashes of the massive Pennsylvania Turnpike, and the squalor of Newark in the sunlight. My memory of the lights of Manhattan in the twilight from Jersey City is still vivid -- we stopped for dinner on the famous island, then made our way eastward. Hobart was parked at JFK Airport until our flight was almost ready to go.

Capitol International Airways' flight crews took excellent care of us before, during, and even AFTER our charter flight to Brussels, Belgium.

I remember a long wait at the terminal while George, and a few others, drove back into the city to store Hobart The Bus. Our charter flight would leave about sunset, and we had all day to ponder the next chapter of our lives and careers. Whatever the other Mime Troupers were doing or thinking, I frankly enjoyed walking the halls of the airport, looking at the modern art with which Governor Nelson Rockefeller and Mayor John Lindsey had stocked the public buildings of New York.

I took turns standing guard over our vast pile of equipment and luggage while others took off to see what they could see. One of the last additions to our prop pile was an oversized sombrero which we'd purchased in Tijuana, Mexico the previous January. "I bet they don't see anything like THAT over there!" We loaded everything onto the conveyor belts, and sighed with relief.

I have no idea what kind of plane we boarded, but remember that there were three seats on either side of a long, long aisle, and many rows of them. The ventilation system was bad at first, but they took care of that by the time we started moving. Our flight crew was totally awe-inspiring! I'd flown before, between Salt Lake and Los Angeles, but that was a very short trip at 600 miles an hour. Our flight attendants were all women, and the term 'stewardess' was rapidly falling into disuse. Somehow they settled a very restive cabin full of tourists with soft words and an ocean's worth of alcohol. Almost everybody on board was asleep after the first hour or so, tucked in with pillows and blankets if they wanted them. The last thing I saw as we flew out of New York City was the relatively new World Trade Center

I enjoyed speaking with curious Europeans and Americans about our theater company, plus the adventures we were facing. I remember sketching a little, and talking with Mark Nelson. The flight attendants were very kind to me, especially when I declined more booze. I ate better than most everyone on the aircraft, and was ready for our landing after a short nap. Matthew Child was our most experienced traveler, and I followed his lead. We were last off the plane, but had everything we needed.

Jet Lag on the train through the Lowlands of Belgium and Holland

Sixteen Troupers got off the plane in Brussels, Belgium and over half of our luggage went on to Frankfurt, Germany. Hoo Boy! David Carrillo was hoping to lay down his temporary leadership after takeoff, but it was not in the cards that day. I lucked out, and got all of my clothes and toiletries back, so there were enough items to keep everyone warm and dry for a few days, with the help of other fortunate individuals. We were still exhausted, disoriented, and jet-lagged -- with an overland journey to The Netherlands ahead of us before we could rest.

Somehow we found our way to the train station, where Mark Nelson and John Fischer bought our tickets and got directions for Amsterdam -- which included a transfer in some city along the way, the name of which I've long forgotten. While we were waiting for the second train, a small foraging party went searching for a nearby grocery store, and luckily found one. A real sit-down meal was welcome to us all!

Unfortunately, the extra energy might have affected some folks' good judgment, and another small group literally went running off to do some sightseeing, despite loud protests from everyone else. Our train came and went, but we had to sit and wait until our impulsive tourists returned before we could do anything at all. Fischer and I then went to the stationmaster's office, and learned that a train with an identical destination was due in an hour, and our tickets were still valid. We were happy for the good fortune, but enduring the long fuming silence in the waiting room was no fun. While daylight remained on the train, I noted how new and modern the houses of Belgium seemed to be, and remembered that the country had been devastated during both World Wars.

It was about 10 PM in Amsterdam when we finally arrived at Centraal Station. We kept the company and remaining luggage close together, and desperately tried to contact our hosts at the 'Milky Way' nightclub. Lord knows -- it's likely we looked like a collection of old rag dolls by then, but a long-haired young man from De Melkweg eventually drove up in a big van, then took us and our possessions to their guest dormitory in De Rosenstraat.

Before we finally went to sleep, we actually went to see the famous club we'd heard so much about from the Friends Roadshow. I remember peeking into the Theater Zaal alongside Katie and watching swirling dancers through a haze of hashish smoke. There were posters everywhere telling who'd performed and when. One especially caught my eye that night -- Nico from the old Velvet Underground had played there previously, and she looked beautiful on the silkscreened image. Any thought that I'd be on the same stage with her a year later never crossed my mind.

We sat down in the Milky Way's restaurant for a much-needed meal. Across the table from me was the friendly face of Ted Van Zutphen ("Dutch Ted"), who we'd met when he was with Friends Roadshow in La Crosse. I told him I was happy to be a guest in HIS country for a change. Katie was excitedly talking to Patsy, saying "We can do anything we want in there," meaning the theater. As we later walked towards the nearby Rosenstraat, Katie smiled through her exhaustion and said: "We're here at last" to Carrillo and myself -- the same two guys who'd initiated this whole thing ten months earlier, along with Jango, at the International Mime Festival.

Trans-Atlantic Coda

Whatever happened to our missing luggage? Capitol International Airways delivered everything to the door of De Melkweg two days later. There was an awfully lot of stuff when it finally arrived, and I frankly hate to think about what COULD have happened had we actually tried to haul it all ourselves between Brussels and Amsterdam. In retrospect, I worship all the goddesses of Capitol for their life-saving intercession on behalf of foolish Troupers like me and my friends.

1975 Festival of Fools and Holland
THE ROAD hops the Atlantic for the Netherlands and places unknown.

Summary: The Great Salt Lake Mime Troupe spent about a month gigging their way from California to Michigan, where they stayed with the Friends Roadshow, and finalized plans for performing in Amsterdam, Holland. After a mad dash to New York City, they parked their bus and boarded a Capitol Airways charter plane. They slept all night under the nurturing gaze of the flight attendants, and shuffled into the Brussels airport at daylight while half their baggage flew on to Frankfurt. Somehow, despite suffering acute jet lag, the whole group made it to Amsterdam by rail. They went immediately to the Milky Way nightclub (De Melkweg), where Capitol delivered the rest of their clothing and equipment two days later.

700 Years of Amsterdam, Holland, and International Friends

Peter Domela Nieuwenhuis was one of the very first people who sought us out at De Melkweg when we finally arrived in Amsterdam. Jango had previously contacted Peter and asked him to "take care" of us. It wasn't quite the same as Strider rescuing the Hobbits from Black Riders in *Lord of the Rings*, but we sure needed his help!

Before I tell any more of this story, I am pausing to thank this kind and giving man for all the efforts he made on our behalf. Now back to the chaos of awaking in a strange country, with half our luggage missing -- Ohan, a Turkish laborer from Germany, acted as dorm-manager for De Melkweg in their loft space on the Rosenstratt. I spoke a little high school German, which helped a lot. Ohan also had a funny-looking dog who scratched himself a bit too much.

There were a few other guests at the Rosenstraat, a fact which might have made some of us uncomfortable, but they were just passers-through like us. Matthew made us all laugh ourselves to tears when he imitated the dog's mannerisms. We WERE concerned about dirt, fleas, and hygiene, but that was a sign of sanity rather than burnout. I was among the lucky Troupers who had kept their clothes, towels, and toiletries. We spread them around the rest of the company.

There was still a dismal vibe amongst most of the group, but we needed to eat, wash up, and find our way around the place we had invested most of a year in reaching anyway. Our first efforts at shopping were pretty laughable in retrospect, but there were plenty of stores in the neighborhood, and Dutch people were used to bewildered tourists. I encountered nothing but smiles on the streets when it was my turn to run errands. We discovered facts like "ei" meant egg, and "gemalen" meant ground coffee.

Peter showed up at the Rosenstraat the very first morning and tried to get our weary aggregation settled. He owned an upstairs floor in a residential building in the west part of the city, which had been vacant for quite a while, and did us the kindest favor possible by opening the place up for our use within the week. After Capitol Airways delivered the rest of our luggage, we moved into Peter's apartment. I cut my elbow on a stray piece of glass while we were cleaning, but Peter drove me to the hospital and gave them his insurance number. They stitched it up right away.

Amsterdam was celebrating its 700th Anniversary. The city was beautiful, for sure, but it took a lot of effort by its residents to keep things clean and in repair.

Peter found transportation for us -- a pleasant Volkwagen microbus, decorated with duck stickers, which soon owned the name Fannius Duck, after our address on Fannius Scholtenstraat. We also got the keys to a smelly VW square-back variant.

We encountered other allies, including the Amsterdam branch of Friends Roadshow. Rather than being performers, they were technicians, artists, and engineers named Cor Francks, Henk Targowski, Charly Jungbauer, and Janet Beevers -- with Charlz Jundo off in Rome for some reason. They owned a fabulous stereo system, and shared my enthusiasm for Reggae music, plus edgy Rock like Captain Beefheart and the Magic Band. We would work with them more and more as the Festival of Fools approached.

Idyll at the Funpark by Gooi Zee

Just as we started to settle in West Amsterdam, Peter led us to the Dutch countryside where we had an opportunity to perform in a "Funpark" near a lake called Gooi Zee. At first Oud Valkeveen seemed idyllic -- everything was clean, neat and painted in dark green, with red and white trim. We had comfortable living quarters not far from the carousel, and the ladies in the kitchen cooked everyone a beautiful meal.

(Left to Right Rear) Chéri; George; Carrillo; Patsy; Mark; Barbara; Peter; Gregg; Stuart; and Jan. (Left to Right Front) Unknown person; Matthew; John; and Michael. Missing from this photo are Katie, Paul, Debra, and Zupan. Image courtesy of Peter Domela Nieuwenhuis

The next day started out with a parade from the nearby village to the amusement park on bikes, unicycles, and slow-moving open trucks. Zupan even juggled astride his bicycle in makeup! The Mime Troupe played music, and the dancers performed a few numbers. George worked his magic on young and old alike. I painted my face too, and had a great time in the early afternoon teaching children how to juggle without understanding a word of their language -- I gradually learned how to count in Dutch that day, though. We had our first rehearsal in Europe at their restaurant, and the owner promptly took an interest in our band -- sitting in on piano.

We stayed at the Funpark for most of a week. On Sunday afternoon, I was sitting down at lunch in the warm May sunshine, surrounded by smiling Dutch ladies my own age, and enjoying the cheers of children I'd been teaching as they passed by us.

Thoughts of the railroad where I had been working just a year before went through my head, and I was glad I'd chosen another life. It seemed almost too good to be true, and so it was -- what started out with such promise turned into a period of crisis during the following days. For one thing we were having too many meetings over too many trivial subjects. Chéri had enough of our precarious lifestyle, so George found her a place elsewhere, and she disappeared from the Mime Troupe's story. Peter warned us that the owner of the Funpark wanted to literally take us over, and he was correct -- as we tried to get ready for our upcoming concerts, the owner tried to convince everyone with influence to abandon the Festival of Fools, particularly De Melkweg. The outlines of his "Dutch Uncle" exhortations spread throughout the group. He especially wanted our band to work for him all summer. When we went to The Hague for our first international concert, we returned to Amsterdam afterwards and never went back to Het Gooi.

The Hot Theater in The Hague

The Hot Theater's festival included David Bowie's teacher Lindsay Kemp, Jango's former partner Nola Rae, and the duo of Byland & Gaulier who we'd seen in La Crosse, Wisconsin the previous year. We saw the Hot Theater for the first time when we traveled there as a group to see Nola Rae and Peter Wyssbrod Biel on their second night, where Biel performed his existential *Abfall* (Garbage) after the intermission following Nola's energetic, yet conservative mime show -- which became progressively better and better over her career. She was also a source of very good advice about the European theater scene, and a sweet lady in every way.

We were ready to do a concert -- bar gigs and street performances were not satisfying any of our needs. Jet lag, bad nerves, and the disorientation from our long trip were still affecting us, but everyone was CONCENTRATING on the first of our two nights -- sometimes so much that the crew had to remind us what time it was, and how soon we were supposed to go on.

The band started playing, and the Great Salt Lake Mime Troupe went about showing the Old World a whole new synthesis of Dance and Mime. I remember the show as dark and intense. Emotions were keyed very high, and Matthew's *Puppet* routine with Carrillo started earlier than normal. The audience was often breathless, and enjoyed the relief of Georgio's gentle clowning. Further emotional storms were released during our Modern Dance sequences. When the concert finished and I raised the house lights, the audience surged onstage and everyone started embracing or shaking hands. We had a lot of supporters from Amsterdam in the crowd, but they weren't the only ones who offered hugs of reassurance and congratulations after our gut-baring performance!

Image of the Hot Mime Festival 1975 poster courtesy of Matthew Child.

I turned my eyes away from the teeming crowd below the lighting booth to turn off the board and get my notes in order for next night. When I looked out again, everybody was sprawled face-down on the floor of the stage. What the heck was going on down there? Ah -- One of our dancers lost a contact lens in the tears and turmoil. Luckily, it was found within minutes.

There was another "first" that night at the Hot Theater: Mark Nelson performed his solo Folk Music act in the lobby during intermission and after the show. Gregg Moore shouted "Let's go dig Mark!" in the dressing room, and we ran down to see him play his dulcimer and sing songs like: *Your daddy was a Basque, drank his liquor from a flask, and he lived out on the range in Eye-dah-HO!*

The next night was even better -- I brightened up the lights, and everyone was more confident by many percentage points. The theater was packed. Word had gotten around that something different was happening, and it was beautiful to see. Whatever moodiness happened onstage the second evening might have come from the music or actors, but not the lights in the hall. Mark's music was very pleasant to hear in the bar afterward -- his jaw harp and harmonica came into play too. He would soon book himself in Amsterdam's Folk Fairport club, and play whenever he could.

De Lantaarn in Rotterdam and Toneelschuur in Haarlem

We had two more concerts booked besides De Melkweg and the rapidly-upcoming Festival of Fools. Our experience in The Hague infused a measure of confidence and energy in the group as a whole which were great antidotes to jet lag and homesickness We were staying at Peter's apartment in the Oud West section of Amsterdam. It was a longer walk to De Melkweg from there, but not an unbearable stroll -- we had a tram stop nearby, and a bicycle or two on hand most of the time. The motor vehicles were available when needed, but converting liters and guilders to gallons and dollars was pretty scary, and we did almost no casual driving.

The best thing for me about the upcoming concerts was that they were close to the train stations in both Rotterdam and Haarlem. I was able to get to them independently, then find the loading zone, arrange for dressing rooms, locate enough microphones and stands for everyone, and arrange lighting before the rest of the Mime Troupe arrived with their own individual needs.

The loading zone in Rotterdam was a total nightmare -- it was off a tiny street, dating from the Middle Ages, and the alleyway was tighter than the road, which almost too narrow for horses. Other than that near-disaster, everything went really well at De Lantaarn. The stage was on the floor like the Hot Theater, thrusted deep into the seats.

The audience enjoyed their intimacy with our attractive performers, but as silliness led to seriousness, and Juggling led to soaring Dance, they alternately held their collective breath and gasped at the Great Salt Lake Mime Troupe's dynamics. There was no mad rush afterward, but dozens of people lingered to communicate their feelings of love and respect. We would soon return to De Lantaarn, but in a different context altogether.

Haarlem's Toneelschuur was more of a youth club, like the Milky Way was supposed to be. They were a much smaller operation, and focused on their goals in a manner which wasn't so widely encompassing. The management and customers sure liked having fun, though! The received our blend of Circus, Mime, and Modern Dance with deep appreciation, but liked our band most of all, and danced for as long as the musicians would play after the main show.

Our band had incorporated Herbie Hancock's electro-funk masterpiece *Chameleon* in their repertory from Aspen onward. His distinctive bass line had been driven by John Fischer's left hand on a spare keyboard, because Gregg Moore played trombone during the long, jazzy number. That night, the public got a load of what we should have been doing months before -- our fabulous guitarist Paul Blackwell took over Gregg's idle bass and drove that sinuous jam like an engineer drives an express train.

De Toneelschuur's technician took over the lighting booth, and threw some dance music on the reel-to-reel machine up there. There was a modern loading dock out back, so we were packed and ready to go in less than an hour. I joined in the dancing on the floor while the rest of the Troupers got dressed and wandered around the venue sipping on good Dutch beer. By the time we were ready to leave, I had shaken my body and sweated away my inhibitions with every woman in the place, and enjoyed goodbye kisses until about 3:30 in the morning.

During the half-hour drive back to Amsterdam, we noticed the sky getting light -- it was grey dawn when we disembarked at Peter's house. We hadn't realized until then how far north we were, and how summer was advancing fast.

The Great Salt Lake Mime Troupe prepares for Amsterdam

There was still much to see and discover about Amsterdam -- learning how to navigate the tramways was fun, as were the open-air markets. We met our friend Jean Paul Bell from Aspen as well -- he was doing *Please Buy My Fleas* to taped accompaniment. Mike Heron was performing at the open-air Vondelpark with his new Rock group. I had enjoyed his solo album, *Smiling Men With Bad Reputations*, as well as almost all of the work he'd done with Robin Williamson in the Incredible String Band.

One of my very favorite songs was *Rainbow*, sung by Malcolm LeMaistre, who was also singing with Heron. I put on my whiteface make-up, grabbed my juggling bag, and went to the show, which had everything I was hoping to hear -- textural Rock Music, emotional lyrics, plus high soulful singing, with hints of Heron's Scottish heritage.

The audience enjoyed his ode to Heavy Rock -- *Warm Heart Pastry*, where he'd previously recruited members of The Who for the thundering background tracks. De Melkweg sponsored the concert, so I had no problem getting backstage.

I introduced myself, and politely invited Mr. Heron and Mr. LeMaistre to our upcoming premiere at the Milky Way. They were quite intrigued when they heard how members of my group and I had seen the Incredible String Band in Salt Lake City during the spring of 1974. "That was a really good show," said Heron, with a broad smile on his face. I reminded LeMaistre of his own Mime performance in Utah -- "Crocodile!" he said with surprise and glee, as Heron laughed.

The ensuing conversation involved hearing how the Incredible String Band broke up in Memphis, Tennessee on the night of Nixon's resignation, while we were celebrating in La Crosse, Wisconsin, at the International Mime Festival, hundreds of miles further up the Mississippi River. "I wish I could have been there," said LeMaistre.

"That festival is the reason we're here right now," I said, and attempted to describe Jango's connection with Amsterdam. I also told Heron and LeMaistre how their music meant a great deal to me in my own life, and the eclecticism found in THEIR art was an important part of OUR art as well. After walking away from two of my musical heroes, I calmed down a bit by juggling -- legally earning some money with a street show.

Amsterdam embraces the Great Salt Lake Mime Troupe

De Melkweg, A.K.A. Milky Way, was once a dairy, but became a complex of theaters and cafes featuring vibrant international Alternative Culture. Even though we had four successful concerts behind us in Holland, the Great Salt Lake Mime Troupe's debut at De Melkweg was still a big deal for us. I was personally confident that we would impress the whole town and become the star attraction of the upcoming Festival of Fools -- whatever our strengths and weaknesses. (Or woeful lack of knowledge about our competition, in my particular case.) We had a show made up of elements which few groups had attempted to gather together before.

With the exception of Peter, nobody had shown more kindness and support than the staff at De Melkweg. Wouter, Cor, Han, Susanne, Suzette, et al. The quality of the people we met there is beyond description -- they welcomed us to a strange country and did everything within their power to make us feel that we had some kind of home. We used their facilities for rehearsal, storage, and relaxation, not to mention the hot showers. By the time our weekend was ready to begin we knew the layout of the space where we were going to perform, and I already had experience with their solid-state lighting board. We had experimented with ideas for new material -- some had stalled, some had succeeded. What we had ready was well-rehearsed and powerful.

There was a bit of an emergency for me to face when I learned that De Melkweg's entire graphics staff were replaced just before our posters were to be printed. I volunteered to help the new artist do his first run, and he accepted. He had a sure hand on his silk-screen squeegee, liking high-contrast images and split-fountain colors, He appreciated having someone to load the drying racks, refresh the inks, and keep the sheets of paper coming as they were needed. For myself, I appreciated hearing the old-timey folk music rising from the bakery's sound system below as I stacked up our graphics. Mark Nelson sang those same tunes in his live act. The posters were long somewhat narrow strips which described a whole week's worth of attractions, but the Mime Troupe was on top of the playbill, where I knew we belonged.

    Our first weekend at the Melkweg (pictured above) was an outright triumph -- the pure beauty of our dances and dancers punctuated the emotional character-driven stories we told in Pantomime. George's low-key modesty turned the audience upside-down with surprise as his juggling skills blew away all their preconceptions. The crazy satire of "Competition" proved that sports mania knew no international boundaries. Another dance sent the audience higher than the second stage of an Apollo rocket. A little more poignant drama set up the emotional climax of John Fischer's rondo with our four best dancers sailing through the air in high leaps, barrel rolls, and circular turns inside a wider circle. I myself "danced" with the lights in that number -- deeply-saturated aqua and blue were the key colors, which would follow our dancers around and around, while I teased a few highlights with warm pinks and rose fresnels at the edges of their faces and figures. As stunned silence turned to wild applause at the conclusion of our concert, I turned around to see Mike Heron and Malcolm LeMaistre smiling, with deep reflective eyes staring right at me. "Beautiful show!" said Heron, and I hugged them both, right then and there.

    I can't remember if we did three or four more concerts that weekend, but there were fewer and fewer places to sit or stand in the Theatre Zaal as time progressed. Every show was a jewel. The only setback we suffered that weekend was a rain-out at the gig scheduled for Vondelpark. Embryo, a German jam-band (with Sean Bergin as a guest) did their best to entertain the hardy souls who stood in the soggy weather while we huddled under a covered stage -- but nobody in the audience, stoned or sober, stayed very long, and the management sent us home so we could be fresh for the show later that night, and perhaps avoid pneumonia.

The Mime Troupe also spent time with Mike Heron and his band. Our musicians jammed with his musicians one afternoon at De Melkweg. Malcolm and Katie talked about the nature of performing. The most amazing time we shared was Heron's concert at De Lantaarn in Rotterdam. The staff even played a black and white video tape of our recent performance in the lobby during intermission. I was seriously moved by his song about the breakup of the Incredible String Band -- *Down On My Knees In Memphis, Down On My Knees*. Heron and his group went onward, with equipment borrowed from Manfred Mann's Earth Band, and we drove back to Amsterdam. I was not really prepared for what happened next.

So what if Neil Sedaka wrote a song about it too -- Breaking up is HARD ...

One morning, at Peter's apartment, soon after the Melkweg concerts were finished, the Great Salt Lake Mime Troupe held the last of our many contentious meetings. Three of our dancers announced that they "couldn't live this way any longer." Many things were said by others, including me, who hated to see our hard work dismantled just as we were beginning to get the recognition we'd sought for so long, but a critical mass of minds were made up, and the group decided to disband after the Festival of Fools. (Important note: The Troupe re-formed within months, and returned to Amsterdam the next year.)

I remembered pondering Joey Grimaldi's ghost-written biography by Charles Dickens, where the great clown described his life as a chain of successes followed by failures, but I didn't ponder long -- after juggling practice in Westerpark, I decided to get back to work -- the Festival of Fools would begin in week, and there was still a hellish amount of labor that needed to be done.

Final Diversion -- Albums from the Amsterdam Friends' collection -- plus one

Catch A Fire by The Wailers had been simmering on store shelves for almost two years, but the ever-growing success of Bob Marley and the Wailers attracted new fans with great songs, like ***Stir It Up***

Clear Spot by Captain Beefheart and the Magic Band boldly strode the line between Avant Garde and Commerciality: ***It's Been Too Much Time (To Be Without Love)***

Mott -- the follow-up to *All The Young Dudes*. I couldn't forget or ignore Ian Hunter's lament about Mott the Hoople's own (temporary) breakup in the song *Ballad Of Mott -- March 26th 1972 Zurich*: *We crossed the mighty oceans and we had a few divides -- But we never crossed emotion for we felt too much inside.*

The 1975 Festival of Fools, and Amsterdam's bountiful harvest of the same

No matter what the Great Salt Mime Troupe had in mind for their collective futures, the Festival of Fools was scheduled, and would happen anyway -- with or without us. Along with preparing for our Melkweg appearance, I worked shoulder to shoulder with Charly, Cor, and Henk as we laid-out and printed the schedule of performances, and workshops for subsequent events which encompassed three different theaters and the streets of that seven hundred year old city.

The late M.C. Escher had a relative who was then currently in charge of all the advertising kiosks in the Centrum of Amsterdam, and Gielijn Escher composed a beautiful logo for the festival. We worked past 3:00 AM for many nights just getting our graphics together and acquiring accurate information for the program. Kirke Wilson amalgamated various fools from various decks of Tarot cards, and Henk adapted carloads of Robert Crumb characters motoring on Amsterdam streets for the covers.

A Teen Age Palm Tree grows at the Shaffy Theater

Once the American Friends arrived in Holland, they had to arrange transportation, housing, and equipment just like us. While we were staying at Friends Farm, Jango and Novotny were working on a special production for the Festival of Fools which bore the name *I was A Teenage Palm Tree*. It was a satire about cheesy monster movies, and film-making in general. The rest of the company was obviously involved too. They brought a couple of new people, including affable Ed Baker as their stage manager, and a man whose name I've forgotten to play the stalking "Palm Tree." The giant Groote Zaal at the Shaffy Theater was the designated venue, so Friends Roadshow and allies like me started to make the idea real.

I had most of the week free before the Great Salt Lake Mime Troupe started performing again, so I asked Michael Novotny what I could do to help him. He sat down and sketched designs for two sets of flats and some artificial waves. The paint and materials were there in the Shaffy already, so I said yes right away. Jango then gave me another task -- build a small city for the monstrous Palm Tree to destroy.

For the next month I spent almost all of my time between De Melkweg and the Shaffy Theater. I slept at Peter's place, but after a quick breakfast and juggling practice at nearby Westerpark, I left to take care of my duties in BOTH buildings for the festival as an entity in itself, as well as my own group.

One set of *Palm Tree*'s flats was to be tropical island scenes, with innocent palm trees leaning in towards center stage, ominously hinting about the predatory sylvan creature lurking in the further jungle. Another set was supposed to evoke a tramp steamer, carrying movie maker *Frederico Fungali* and his crew to a legendarily haunted tropical paradise *ala* King Kong.

Novotny played *Fungali* with Italianate *brio*, and relied on a crew of *azoles* to get things done -- like shifting our curly-cue waves back and forth manually, while the *Palm Tree* stealthily chucked deadly coconuts all around them. His cast of *azoles* thinned out FAST.

As the Friends Roadshow rehearsed their songs, and worked out their special effects, I put my Art School training to use -- sketching out the "Tropical Flats" and putting them aside since they required a lot of detail work. I borrowed a slide projector from Henk and Charly, plus a number of slides Henk had made of Amsterdam streets, then made yards of paper buildings that I could turn into a little city doomed to destruction. The first scenes I finished were the "Boat Flats" -- port holes, glass, rivets, and heavy doors were easy for me to draw, with just enough cast-shadows to make them look good under theatrical lights. I even used my sable brush from Denver!

I worked hard and fast. Jango dropped in on me one night by surprise and seeing that the Boat Flats were done, the Doomed City was ready to fold, and the Tropical Flats were drafted with days to spare, he said "That's REALLY good, Mike!"

A compliment from Jango was very welcome, of course, but good fortune had already blessed our efforts when Ellen Beier began assisting me soon after the project began. She came to Amsterdam from London, along with her pals Nancy, Maggie, and two musicians named Alan and Linda, the latter whom I wouldn't meet for another year. Ellen was a sensitive painter, took over one Tropical Flat and helped paint the waves according to Novotny's designs.

Suzette Bronkhorst (right) from De Melkweg befriended the Mime Troupe as we shuffled back and forth between gigs. That's me on the left, as we worked together during the festival.

I insisted on finishing one of the Tropical Flats myself, starting in my own rather hard-edged University of Utah style, but Ellen's Tropical Flat was much softer, nicer, and more detailed -- I studied what she did, and modified mine to be in harmony with her significant improvements.

Young Scotsman Alan Purves made a short trip back to England, and came back to Amsterdam hauling a massive drum kit. Paul Holland, drummer for the London Friends, recommended him to Ced Curtis, Since the American Roadshow needed someone on the percussive throne very badly, Curtis gave him a chance, and Alan turned out to have real talent. I was dancing in the audience throughout his first gigs, and wasn't at all shy about complimenting him for reaching deep into the pocket of Funk from whence all of Friends Roadshow's music flowed. Ellen became a book illustrator, and Novotny eventually took his talents to the movie industry in Southern California.

Festival of Fools -- Paradiso, Shaffy, Melkweg, and on the street!

The Festival of Fools finally began with a parade across town from Dam Square to the Paradiso, The London Friends performed an original puppet play in Dam Square, an outdoor performance of *Michael Spaghetti's Circus* next to the Paradiso, plus a few indoor joint shows with their old mates from America. I never met more than HALF of this talented communal clan.

As the festival actually began in famous Dam Square around the London Friends' mobile stage, there was a lot going on elsewhere throughout the gigantic cobble stone plaza as well -- Michael Novotney and Rick Parets went around dressed as *Alfie* and *Professor Felix Varoom*, clowning about, and dropping a pair of pants or two. I was smiling and juggling between various acts, and joined the parade, resting at De Paradiso, a Rock venue adapted from an old church. In those days, the place featured a busy, but brilliant light show that went on constantly -- especially between featured entertainers. They played clips from old cowboy movies, cartoon segments, kaleidoscopic pools of oil and liquid, and superimposed slides from all sorts of crazy subject matter.

Later that evening, the action started with the Rock band Sail, featuring Jo-Alice Banra, and Justin's mom Karen Harvey, followed by Michael "Madness" Novotny -- introducing the American Friends as they kicked up a high-energy revue which included members of the London company, and even the Mime Troupe. Paradiso's technical crew didn't need my help, so there was nothing better to do than observe the fun. Friends Band was especially dazzling on Marvin Gaye's *Inner City Blues* -- with an arrangement straight off the Grover Washington Jr. album we'd all heard at Friends Farm. Original Friends tunes like *Industrial Love* got everybody danc-ing, and Rick brought on more laughs singing *If Ya' Got Papers, Ya' Ain't Got Dope...*

There were some more moments when I reflected how far I'd come from the suburbs of Salt Lake City, Utah -- especially when Rick, Ted, and Carl strode out wearing glittery outfits and glasses as a Glam-Rock group named "Puke." Glam-Rock was a bit passé, but still selling, and when the three androgynous singers belted out *Wild Thing*, I knew my politician father would NOT approve of my career anytime soon -- if ever. Jango took over the show early, and the audience loved every joke he made.

Great Salt Lake Mime Troupe's new home venue at the Shaffy Theater

The Great Salt Mime Troupe helped the Friends Roadshow get *I was a Teen Age Palm Tree* going in the Groote Zaal on the first floor of the Shaffy Theater, but it was still THEIR show, and would succeed or fail based on what they did. One song was fun and interesting: *Making movies is an art! It's not like sex, it's not so clean. It's all for fun, it's all for crap, and (Fungali) is the loneliest chap!* Some things worked well, and some things didn't -- destroying the little city was funnier to talk about rather than see, and that riff was cut from the show after a couple of fizzles.

The Great Salt Lake Mime Troupe was working two stories further upstairs at the Shaffy, and I didn't have the time to paint anymore towns anyway. Charlz Jundo's slides of jungles and creatures came and went quickly too. There weren't as many *azoles* for *Fungali* to order around as he'd expected, but *Palm Tree* developed a flow over the summer, and even the absurd "cannibal sandwich" routine eventually worked itself out.

Where was the Great Salt Lake Mime Troupe? At the top, of course!

The Great Salt Lake Mime Troupe still danced as well as anyone in the big city. Our band was still damn good, and everyone performed their hearts out during the Festival of Fools. Hundreds made the long climb to the third floor of the Shaffy just to witness the beauty of our show, and were well-rewarded by the experience. I'll admit to some occasional goof-ups, but nobody gave up on their art, no matter how they might have felt about one another or the circumstances.

Katie as her character "Madame Duck" in 1975. (Photo by Ellen Beier)

The Shaffy Zaal was painted a deep twilight blue, festooned with five-pointed stars which gradually clustered closer and closer towards the south side -- we were actually performing inside a painting done by popular Dutch keyboardist Thijs Van Leer from the Progressive Rock group *Focus*.

Standing screens covered the busy stellar climax and star-shaped door. There was plenty of room for musicians and dancers on the floor stage, and the seating was comfortable. Best of all, there was none of the Hashish smoke which had made De Melkweg so fun for the audience, but so tiring for us. We did our best work breathing fresh air. We weren't all living at Peter's anymore either -- the imminent parting of our ways was on everyone's mind.

Everybody knows that Amsterdam is famous for legal cannabis in many forms, so I'm going to tell ONE story about that scene. Near the start of the Festival of Fools, "Foxy," the baker of "Space Cake" at the Melkweg, announced he was going to make his special "Grass Candy" recipe one morning. I worked a particularly long hard day at the Shaffy afterwards. When I finally went downstairs, there were several colleagues complaining about being too high from Foxy's "treat," and how rueful they felt about performing later. As I walked towards De Melkweg in the luscious afternoon light of summer, I met several clusters of friends and acquaintances having obvious difficulties getting back to work, and not knowing whether to laugh or cry about their situation. Nobody in the Mime Troupe got the "opportunity" to try Foxy's candy, and we did a very good show. Somehow, I never asked anybody who had been bitten back by their "sweet tooth" how well that particular night went for them.

Performing in the ruins of Brederode Castle

One of the Great Salt Lake Mime Troupe's last, and more interesting, venues in the summer of 1975 was outdoors in the courtyard of a ruined castle south and east of Amsterdam. The place was named Brederode (pronounced Bray-Dah-Roh-Dah). Rob Weber of the Shaffy Theater accompanied us, and helped me set up my American lights for the second and final time in Europe. We also utilized some colored spotlights strung on the eldritch trees to help decorate that old pile of stone at night.

The audience sat on folding chairs, blankets on the ground, and even improvised lounges on the walls. They were all associated with a psychiatric school and clinic in a nearby town. They saw some character-mime, and a little dancing -- the uneven ground was too hazardous for our longer set-pieces. Georgio was as entertaining as ever, but I still wondered what this particular audience was thinking as they watched, because we were NOT concealing our feelings that night.

Friends Roadshow performed there the next year, and Tumbleweeds from San Francisco played that gig in 1977. All three of us were sprawling multi-disciplinary amalgamations of musicians and performers -- make up your OWN mind!

Foots Barn Theatre asked me to join their upcoming tour in England

With the Mime Troupe's imminent disbanding coming closer, I wanted to find another job. We had made contact with Foots Barn Theatre while we were at Friends Farm, and discussed a potential "rural tour" with them during the upcoming summer. I mentioned to Michael Novotny that I was "looking for another gig," and asked if Foots Barn could use another hand with their new tent. He thought for a moment and advised me to speak with them directly. It wasn't very long before we were all sitting in the offices of the Milky Way, and I immediately made my case to the five friendly strangers sitting around me. A few days later, after one of my solo street shows, Steve Lawrence stepped up and invited me to join the company -- I accepted gladly!

Many kinds of farewells, regroupings, and De Kosmos

The Festival of Fools reached its end on the 22nd of June in 1975. There was no big celebration or ceremony that year. The Friends Roadshow was heading off to La Rochelle, France. Carrillo and Zupan went along as official members, plus the latter enrolled for fall classes at Dimitiri's school in Ticino, Switzerland. Gregg managed to stay in Europe that summer too. George and Mark decided to go to Dublin, Ireland, where an Art Center hired them for a few weeks. They combined their talents and worked out some routines together, but Nelson concentrated on music after returning to the USA.

Upper Left: David Zupan in France after the 1975 Festival of Fools with variously amalgamated Friends Roadshow members and friends of Friends; Center Top: Ted Van Zutphen, Dave Carrillo; From Middle Left; Michael Novotney, Helena Van Danzig; From Lower Right: Lenny Kovner, Ed Baker, Suzette Bronkhorst, Marshall Erskine, Paul Holland.

Patsy, Matthew, John, Stuart, Debra, Paul and Jan went directly to the United States. Katie stayed in Europe, and even worked with Friends Roadshow. In fact, there was one post-festival Mime Troupe show at a club called De Kosmos which was one of the few times they played without her since the founding of the group. I wasn't there myself, because of my spending time with a Dutch lady named Neeltje. We met in one of my juggling workshops during the Festival, and would be together for the next two years.

What is there to say about my trip to England? I rode the so-called "Magic Bus" with Alan and Nancy from the Museumsplein in Amsterdam to Vlissingen (Flushing) Holland, and boarded a ferry about sunset. At daybreak we disembarked at Sheerness at the mouth of the Thames River where I got my passport stamped with an ironic notice saying I was forbidden to do any paid or unpaid work. There was a nice conversation on the train into London with a young English lady who guided my steps through Victoria Station and on to Paddington, where the westbound railroad eventually crossed over I.K. Brunel's mighty Saltash Bridge into Cornwall -- the first thing I saw when reaching the seaside was a PALM TREE, hopefully an omen of good fortune!

Trans-Channel Coda

When I got off the train at Liskeard, I called Steve Lawrence -- Paddy Haytor, Joe Cunningham, and he drove up from their farm at Trewen, and took my luggage and me to Elsie's Red Lion Pub for a beer. There was a live parrot holding court out of a second floor window across the street. When we finally got back to Trewen, my first task was helping to paint a banner for the top of Foots Barn's new tent.

And that lady from London? She showed up with a few friends in St. Ives to see Foots Barn's show about a month later. Neeltje also came to see us at the end of the tour, and accompanied me to Holland on vacation. After we eventually relocated to Amsterdam, I continued to help Footsbarn whenever they came to play, and vice-versa. John Kilby came on board to lend his capable hand to managing the group. These talented people have been very good friends to me over the years.

We met again at the World Theatre Festival in Denver, Colorado during the blistering hot summer of 1982. They had come to the USA with The *Doctor, The Devil, and The Fool*, a spectacle based on the primordial imagery of medieval mummer's plays -- under the folds of a huge circuslike tent. Footsbarn were the hit of the festival. The timeless pageantry created a spell that bewitched their audiences, stirring thoughts and emotions to a depth almost unknown to American theater-goers, but appreciated for that very reason. After leaving Trewen, they endured ten hard years without a permanent home base. Footsbarn Theatre finally settled in central France. They have visited every populated continent, and I was part of their 35th Anniversary Celebration in 2006.

Primary Documents from 1975

Plate Seven:
US Passport (1975 to 1980)

Matthew Child was an accomplished photographer, and more than one picture in this book was shot through his 35mm reflex camera. During our hectic preparations in Salt Lake City after the California tours in 1975 he made sure we all had good snapshots for our passports. (Page 95)

Plate Eight::
Permit from the City of Amsterdam for Street Theater
Signed by the Office of the Mayor

Amsterdam law rarely permitted Street Theater, although they had an annual "anything goes" Royal Birthday celebration on the streets for 24 hours every spring. However, the Festival of Fools managed to swing this blanket permit for our lunacy day and night. I had a couple of juggling scenarios ready to perform, and the cash came in very handy. One of my colleagues still got busted for "begging," but he kept the money under his hat, stayed quiet, and took it all home. (Page 96)

GEMEENTE AMSTERDAM
Stadhuis, Oudezijds Voorburgwal – Telefoon 21 44 55

No. S. 21722
524/128 A.Z.1975

~~Betreft: openbare vermakelijkheden.~~

DE BURGEMEESTER VAN AMSTERDAM,
Gezien een adres waarbij namens C. Schlösser, projectleider van de Stichting Melkweg, kantoorhoudende Lijnbaansgracht 234A alhier, blijkens nadere toelichting vergunning wordt verzocht in de periode van 6 tot en met 22 juni 1975, op de tussen 10.30 en 22.30 uur en op de zondagen tussen 13 en 22.30 uur op de openbare weg in deze gemeente door diverse groepen toneel- en muziekuitvoeringen te doen geven en daarbij incidenteel gebruik te maken van een rijdend-uitklapbaar podium alsmede van een geluidsinstallatie met twee luidsprekers;

Gelet op art. 3 der Zondagswet;

Gelet voorts op art. 97, onder a en b, in verband met art. 6, 4e lid, der Algemene Politieverordening van Amsterdam;

~~Geeft te kennen dat het verzoek wordt toegestaan, onder voorwaarde:~~

dat op de zondagen in geen geval voor 13 uur vermakelijkheden worden gegeven;

dat voor elk optreden tijdig contact wordt opgenomen met het betrokken politie-district alsmede tijdig overleg wordt gepleegd met de afdeling Beplantingen van de Dienst der Publieke Werken, Kamerlingh Onneslaan 3 alhier (tel. 35.96.66) voor wat betreft het optreden in parken;

dat de aanwijzingen van de politie, betrekking hebbende op de geluidssterkte van de geluidsinstallatie, stipt worden opgevolgd;

dat op eerste vordering van de politie het gebruik van de geluidsinstallatie, onmiddellijk wordt gestaakt;

dat door middel van de geluidsinstallatie geen reclame voor firma's of zaken, in welke vorm ook, wordt gemaakt;

dat schade als gevolg van het gebruik van deze vergunning, toegebracht aan gemeente-eigendommen, op eerste vordering van gemeentewege, door de houder dezer vergunning, wordt vergoed;

dat tijdens de vertoningen door buitenlandse groepen een vertegenwoordiger van genoemde stichting aanwezig is, die als zodanig voor ambtenaren van politie kenbaar is en de mogelijkheid heeft om eventuele bevelen van de politie door de deelnemers te doen naleven;

Herinnert belanghebbende eraan:

dat de bepalingen van wet en verordening, in het bijzonder van de verordening op de heffing van een belasting op vermakelijkheden, moeten worden nageleefd;

dat geen aanspraak op schadevergoeding kan worden gemaakt indien door de Burgemeester sluiting van vermakelijkheden wordt bevolen.

Deze vergunning moet onverwijld aan het kantoor der gemeentebelastingen, James Wattstraat 84 alhier, worden getoond.
O/Kn
Leges

Amsterdam, 6 juni 1975
De Burgemeester voornoemd,

Samkalden

Afschr.

Amsterdam's Festival of Fools -- 1975

Melkweg, Paradiso, and Shaffy created an alternative to the Holland Festival.

Various groups pitched in together to introduce the festival to Amsterdam

Friends Charly and Hank organized the printing of the program, as info and images dribbled in from the business offices. I lent a hand with some artwork, but mostly cranked the Gestetner machine and collated pages.

Art by Kirke Wilson, who wrote in 2011: "I was in fact, producing the Melkweg programs with the Gestetner at that time and am the artist who drew the cover of the various fools from the Tarot decks I researched at American Discount Bookstore (now called The American Book Center)."

Besides my backstage work and street performances, I taught juggling classes in the Fonteinzaal of the Melkweg, and was very surprised when Jango stuffed a small wad of Guilders into my hand for payment -- didn't know if we were making any money at all with the Fool's School. Katie's classes did well and compliments were frequent too -- Amsterdam was learning something. The London Friends performed their rousing Michael Spaghetti's Circus from their mobile stage, parked outdoors next to the Paradiso in the evening of Saturday, June 7. They did a puppet play and hosted a variety show on Dam Square during the afternoon of Friday, June 6.

After leading the big Fools Parade through downtown Amsterdam, the musicians from the English Friends performed a combined show with the American Friends on opening night inside the Paradiso along with some members of the Mime Troupe.

Ka' Theatre and the Mime Troupe were scheduled at the same time, but one company or the other often started late at the Shaffy -- thank goodness, otherwise I wouldn't have been able to see any segments of their incredible show. (It's possible we started early too, but I kind of doubt THAT!) I saw Justin Case perform for the first time in a duo named Chaos. G.T. Moore and his Reggae Guitars were last on the schedule, but although we danced our collective butts off to their music, they weren't really the final act of the festival.

Kirke further wrote about 1975's program: *... Henk did the Crumb collage and I believe it was Mick Flaum who hand lettered the Fools program. Mick and I were responsible for the silkscreened week, theater and Vondelpark posters for a number of years. Henk Langeveld (RIP - 2011) printed the the Teenage Palm Tree poster.*

Kirke Wilson (RIP - 2013) later collaborated with the Ins and Outs Press

Did the program document exactly what happened and when? Of course not! What kind of fool would say anything like that -- or believe it? It was mostly true, however, but missed a couple of late-night spontaneous shows and jams which were the REAL highlights of the Festival of Fools -- but they weren't planned, so how could they be printed ahead of time? Although there was no single finale in 1975, the strength of what occurred manifested itself in the Amsterdam theater scene for many years afterward.

The author urges all readers to peruse the online collection of

Festival of Fools programs in full color at:

https://amsterdamfools.wordpress.com

Listings for the 1975 Festival of Fools included:

Abracadabra, Bob Carrol, Carlos Trafic, Chaos, Drie Ewerfschande, Embryo, Foots Barn Theatre, Friends Amsterdam, Friends England, The Great Salt Lake Mime Troupe, G.T. Moore and the Reggae Guitars, Gijs Hekrick's Band, Hobbit, Isotope, Jazz O Matic Four, John Bull, Joop Scholten, Kabini, Ka' Theater, Onafhankelijk Toneel, Penta Theatre, Resistente Orkest, Sail, Sedalia Flower Ragtime Orchestra, Slumberland Band, Szmulewitz, Styx (A European group), Theo Lovendie, Volkssalon en Amusements Orkest, Waste of Time, and White Dreams, featuring choreographer and dancer Graziella Martinez.

After the 1975 Festival of Fools, George Kugler performed at Barsham Fair in southeast England before going to Edinburgh. Actor and musician Johnny Melville met Georgio on the grounds, where they became lifelong friends.
Photo by Warwick Moreton of the London Friends Roadshow

Amsterdam's Festival of Fools -- 1976

The freewheeling festival expanded and endured through another decade.

The Great Salt Lake Mime Troupe were stars at the Festival of Fools in 1976

Summary: The Great Salt Lake Mime Troupe formed themselves at the University of Utah in the wake of a Mime workshop by Daniel Sonkin. The core of the group were talented students from the U of U's strenuous Dance Department. They were intrigued with the idea of combining ancient pantomime techniques with goofy slapstick and the open road of untried visual modernity into a unique expression of Modern Dance. This vision also attracted musicians and visual artists like myself. We supported each other through one ambitious show after another. At the International Mime Festival in 1974 we met the Friends Roadshow and Stan Edwards, who invited us to perform in Europe the next year -- which was to be a long year indeed. After forming a Jazz quintet and joining forces with juggler George Kugler, the Mime Troupe proved themselves on the road in Colorado, Utah, California, and Michigan. They validated themselves as entertainers, and as a first-rate dance company, on their first tour of Holland. Unfortunately, the long road to artistic success had affected everybody, one way or another, and the company scattered after the first Festival of Fools -- however it was only a short hiatus, and they regrouped for the Edinburgh Festival in August of 1975.

The Great Salt Lake Mime Troupe triumphed in Utah before they returned to Amsterdam's Festival of Fools

Katie in her clown role "Stubby," pictured in the Salt Lake Tribune as they reported about the Great Salt Lake Mime Troupe's concert at prestigious Kingsbury Hall in 1976.

Rear cover of introductory program for the Festival of Fools in 1976
Image by Henk Langeveld

    The Great Salt Lake Mime Troupe were performing in Salt Lake City again by the fall of 1975. Daniel Robert got his money back for La Crosse, and Hobart the Bus returned to the road -- somehow winding up in the hands of Friends Roadshow guitarist Ced Curtis and drummer Tom Derry for awhile. George later told me that the Mime Troupe gave New Orleans a try, but it wasn't productive enough to stay. However, Carrillo left the company to join a musical group in the so-called Crescent City.

The Troupe also did two shows at the Utah State Prison that year, reformed their band, re-recruited Matthew Child, and hired Alan (Gunga) Purves as their drummer when they returned to the Netherlands that spring.

The Great Salt Lake Mime Troupe's show relied on a lot more verbal comedy and clowning, plus Alan hit the drum kit hard -- he'd played for Friends Roadshow in 1975, and would later join Sail-Joya and sit on the throne for quite awhile. The band was otherwise the same as '75 until later that summer. Debra Ryals was back as a dancer, and Dave Zupan, fresh from Dimitri's school in Switzerland, performed in a new Siamese Twins configuration with Georgio. Matthew and Katie introduced themselves with choreography by Patsy, who stayed in Salt Lake. They had a fabulous summer touring Europe after the Festival of Fools in 1976. The talented Jan Jaap Dekker was their stage manager/artist/photographer during this time. He also designed the logo below.

After a trip to France and Italy in early summer, I was a welcome guest at my old haunts from the previous year. Rob Weber at the Shaffy issued me a Medewerker card, and all doors flew open. It was nice to re-introduce myself to hilarious actor/director Carlos Trafic and singer Joanie Borgman of Blue Rose, who'd seen me and Footsbarn in Mousehole, Cornwall the previous summer. There was a film crew at many performances -- I vividly remember abstract Argentinian stylist Benito Gutmacher playing to the camera in the Zuilenzaal at the Shaffy Theater. I later found out that it was Jacques & Ann Katmor, Victor Ken and "twelve other Israeli cinematogues" making a movie called "The Fools," which was shown at the 1978 Festival.

Letterhead image by Jan Jaap Dekker

The Mime Troupe reduced their numbers drastically at the end of the summer. Ryals, Zupan, and Blackwell were let go, and the band formally split from the Mime Troupe. Katie started doing work on her own throughout Europe. Troupers Georgio, Matthew, and new dancer Barbara Doherty, from the University of Utah, migrated between Europe and the United States, but were back in Amsterdam by early 1977. The band finally named itself *Expression* -- playing in Switzerland, Sweden, and Germany.

Davey Norket was leading the band for Friends Roadshow once more, with new drummer Tom Derry, ace percussionist Linda Anton Curtis, and soundman David Roe, alongside Sean Bergin, Ced Curtis, and Jane Hunt. The steady Ed Baker and Ted Van Zutphen also returned. Bobby Clark joined Michael Novotny, Rick Parets, and Carl Holmer up front, and Jango Edwards led the onstage insanity.

Performers for the 1976 Festival of Fools included:

The USA Friends Roadshow, The Great Salt Lake Mime Troupe, Two Penny Circus, Mime Troupe of America, Mike Lynch as "Piro" or "River," "Friends In High Places" by the London Friends, Theatre Slapstique, Nola Rae's London Mime Company, Crystal Theatre, Chaos, Attic Theatre, Headless Wonder, Abrakadabra, Annie Stainer, Heathcote Williams (a poet), The Sandista Sisters, The Fabulous Poodles, Budgie, the late lamented Thin Lizzy, George Melly, John Chilton's Footwarmers (30's music), Gonzales (Latin big band), Lol Coxhill, Amsterdam's Mimeliga, Carlos Trafic, Benito Gutmacher, Graciella Martinez and White Dreams, Anna and Carlos in Powder Theatre, Hauser Orkater, Dogtroep, Penta Theater, and Funhouse. There were also some amazing films from Pat Duffy, Stan Laurel, Oliver Hardy, Harry Langdon, Snub Pollard, and other great comic actors.

The London Friends Roadshow and their mobile stage are surrounded by Fools in 1976. This image was used on the back cover of the Festival of Fools 1977 introductory program.

Amsterdam's Festival of Fools -- 1977

By then, the Holland Festival faced quality competition for artistry and audiences.

The Great Salt Lake Mime Troupe and the Third Festival of Fools

The Great Salt Lake Mime Troupe relied on Barbara Doherty, Matthew Child, and Katie Duck again for brilliant dancing, plus Georgio for dynamic comedy. They started performing with a greater variety of musicians, mostly because *Expression* had it's own schedule. Some veteran Mime Troupe players were on their own, and available, plus there were other great accompanists/composers around Amsterdam

Gielijn Escher's Foolish Moon logo remained unchanged from 1975 through 1978. The designs varied in 1979, 1980, 1982, and 1984.

Cellist Ernst Reijseger was a potent addition to the ensemble, he also accompanied Ka-tie for a few years. Alan (Gunga) Purves, Sean Bergin, Gregg Moore, and Paul Blackwell often performed with the Mime Troupe.

I was stage manager/lighting technician again for the summer of 1977. Besides the now-traditional Melkweg, Shaffy, and Paradiso, the festival included venues elsewhere in Amsterdam, plus performances in Utrecht, Delft and Nijmegen. The kick-off at De Paradiso was a million laughs -- I made one of my very few appearances with Friends Roadshow that night, and a video of me ran on Dutch TV during the news, from when I marched in the Fools Parade earlier that day. Muyei Power, a fabulous Masoka group from Senegal kept everybody dancing late with clattering drums, electric guitars, and exuberant singing.

Footsbarn Theatre was performing an original play called "The Dancing Bear," which was rich and deep, as well as funny. Somehow, their winter pantomime "Peter Pan" was wrongly touted in the programs. Nola Rae, our "cover girl" on the first week's program, eventually earned the honor of "Commander of the British Empire" for her magnificent theatrical work.

Paul Holland, drummer of Friends Roadshow, wrote musical charts which made Friends Big Band possible, and their music sounded like sheer heaven when played by a full Jazz Orchestra, staged by beautiful Helena Van Danzig and her husband.

Some of Friends Big Band -- with musicians from several groups, including Gregg Moore (top left); Stuart Curtis (right edge); Ted Bunting (center front), Harvey Wainapel (below Moore).

Carlos Trafic and free agent Katie also worked together in those days and showed their stuff during the Festival. These two actors brought out the best in everyone who played with them.

History touched down at the Paradiso Friday night when New York's Richard Hell led Television, arguably the first Punk Rock band. They appeared along with Blondie, fellow veterans of CBGBs. (Talking Heads opened the 4th Festival of Fools a year later.)

We were in Delft throughout Friday, though, performing on a double bill with dancer/mime Annie Stainer and her husband, the late great Reg Bolton. On Saturday night, Annie stopped by the Concertzaal at the Shaffy to see the Great Salt Lake Mime Troupe in one of its LAST performances with a full-scale Jazz band. Katie's choreography for Stu Goldberg's *Lotus Feet* was so beautiful it hurt the eyes -- tears were falling everywhere. Afterward, we moved upstairs to the Shaffy's Zuilenzaal, and shared a magical night with the Los Angeles Mask Theater and Steve Hansen, the Puppet Man. The program called him Steve Hensen, but he always let that slide.

I witnessed Tumbleweeds' impressive debut in the Shaffyzaal, and Spiderwoman's *Lysistrada Numbah*. Franz Josef Bogner's Jazz-like movement and comedy made some fine clowning. Hans Dulfer was an excellent saxophonist, and his daughter Candy Dulfer became world-famous playing the same instrument. She was still a young girl when she first sat in with teacher/bandleader Rosa King -- who played Funk and Jazz just around the corner from the Melkweg and performed at the Fools Festival too.

When the Great Salt Lake Mime Troupe went to Nijmegen, we filled a spacious indoor theater with a young appreciative audience and saturated them with Modern Dance all evening to the electrifying music from Paul Blackwell's guitar and Ernst Rijseger's cello. After the Festival of Fools, Patsy and Debra came to Amsterdam to dance with Katie in a group called Goma Fewtet, with Ernst Reijseger and Sean Bergin.

Performers at the 1977 Festival of Fools included:

Carrousel, Figurentheater Triangel, Dog Troep, The Bamsisters, Onafhankelijk Toneel, Pigeon Drop (founded by members of the Mime Troupe of America), Duo Triplex, Neif Diederik, Barry Nooy, Hans Dulfer and de Perikels, Leopoldo Mastelloni, Shusha and Band, Geoff Cavender Band, Michael Drobny, Muyei Power, Theatre Slapstique, Footsbarn Theatre, Salatka Balloon Band, Action Space, Abrakadabra, John Mellville and Kaboodle, Nola Rae, Justin Case, Colin Barron, Annie Stainer, Bob Kerr's Whoopie Band, Deaf School, Johnny Rondo Trio, Lol Coxhill, Colin Scot, USA Friends Roadshow, Great Salt Lake Mime Troupe, Los Angeles Mask Theatre, Spider Woman, Tumbleweeds, Zupe, Otto, Steve Hansen, River/Piro, Chris Torch, Archie Shep, Friends Big Band, Expression, Theatre Du Matin, Companie du Pot aux, Roses, Arch de Noe, Philippe Duval, Franky and Goa, Carlos Trafic, Le Grand Reveur, Powder Theatre, Benito Gutmacher, White Dreams, Szmulewitz, F.J. Bogner, Horselips, and Mick Flynn.

Amsterdam's Festival of Fools -- 1978

Shifting changes, more expansion, and the last year of annual festivals.

The Great Salt Lake Mime Troupe, Peter Wear, and Available Jelly

Pete Wear, formerly of Theatre Slapstique, joined in the Great Salt Lake Mime Troupe during 1978 with Georgio, Matthew, and Barbara. The band consisted of Gregg Moore, Jimmy Sernesky, and Stuart Curtis, and dubbed themselves Available Jelly. My very last video for the Great Salt Lake Mime Troupe was shot at Kingsbury Hall on the University of Utah campus during the spring of 1978.

The Mime Troupe toured around the Western USA, played at the fourth Festival of Fools, Avignon, Lubijana, and other prestigious venues. For awhile, the Mime Troupe was accompanied by dancer Hillary Elmore, who later toured with Katie (and Footsbarn Theatre) in Tunisia. Katie met cellist Tristan Honsinger about that time and gradually relocated to Florence, Italy. Pete left the group later that year, and Georgio started working with Jack "Otto" Millet, Sharon Landau, and others.

Peter (Batman) Wear and George (Third Base) Kugler performing their scenario "Third Base on the Moon" in the USA. Photo Courtesy of Pete Wear

Peter Wear writes in 2010:

I've been racking my brains but can recall remarkably little of the shows we did. Georgo was always a hit and the band were great. Matt and Barb's dances were controversial -- I remember him sticking his head up the back of her skirt which didn't go down well somewhere, maybe a school. In L.A. at an outdoor show, I decided to upstage everyone by reading a newspaper at the side of the stage and then I set fire to it, burning my trousers too. Can't imagine what I thought I was doing. The items were all very much individual pieces and there was little collaboration.

The Festival of Fools went international in 1978 when various companies performed in Bochum, Germany over a long weekend. Memorabilia courtesy of Jimmy Sernesky.

On Sunday June 11, 1978 another band from New York's Punk-Rock nexus CBGB's appeared onstage at the Paradiso after Friends Roadshow International's "Billy Spears," with Michael Novotny as Master of Ceremonies. The group was named Talking Heads, and would eventually enter the Rock and Roll Hall of Fame.

Performers booked at the 1978 Festival of Fools included:

(According to the program) Pigeon Drop, Sam Angelico and the Busby Berkleys, Bamsisters, Tom Fools Theatre Living Poem Theatre, Loose Ends, Kaboodle, Footsbarn Big Band, Sandineta Fools Band, Three Black and Three White Refined Minstrels, Available Jelly, Onk Termick, Wespe Theater, De Vuilharmonie (Harmony of Garbage, a one man band), Trumbunich Mimes, Talking Heads, Spiderwoman, Carrousel, Long Green Theatre (Reg Bolton and Annie Stainer) Ploink, Justin Case, Johnny Melville, The People Show, Hot Sauce, Geoff Cavendish Band, Fools Jam with Jan Jacobs, Murder Brothers, Carlos Trafic, Katie Duck, Franz Josef Bogner, Michael Gimpel and the Handlangers Crime Caberet, Riciotti, Hare Majesteit, Impulsetheater, Nola Rae, Peter Wear, Zvika Fiszon, Footsbarn Theatre, Friends Roadshow, Abrakadabra, Exile One, Sail-Joia, Kaboodle, Hauser Orkater, Gwendal, Cunning Stunts, Panem et Circenses, Philippe Duval, Foolsband (Ernst Jansz), The Moving Picture Show, and The Phantom Captain Mime Machine.

The Festival of Fools in England -- 1979

Festival of Fools' management announced it would become a bi-annual event after 1978, so there was no festival in Amsterdam during 1979, but Footsbarn organized a Festival of Fools On Tour in England, and printed the program in blue ink on white.

As co-producer John Kilby tells it: *Friends Roadshow performed in Penzance, there was also a concert by the Master Musicians of Jajouka from Morocco. They wanted 250 Pounds to perform. We couldn't afford it, but said they could come and pass the hat. Jajouka produced some magical music and vibes and picked up 260 Pounds. It rained most in Woolacombe (near Torrington). Old Testament rain -- we spent the night as refugees in a local church hall. Exeter was a bit of a blur for me, as it was co-organised by Shirley Jones of 'The Magic Bus.' The weather was better -- a relief as we were under the cosh after Woolacombe. There were a couple of tents and several events in town, in the open air. Bobby Bullethead did a bike jump but without Alfie. "The Greatest Show On Legs" was a highlight. Martin Soan and the wonderful Malcolm Hardee -- he went on to be a bit of a star, but sadly died a couple of years ago.*

Performers booked at the *Festival of Fools On Tour* in 1979 included:

According to the program -- Footsbarn Theatre Company, The Busby Berkleys, The Barneys Theater Company (A Footsbarn spin-off), Clapperclaw, The Moving Picture Show, Sail-Joia, The Lemmings, Great Salt Lake Mime Troupe, Greatest Show On Pants, Incubus Theatre Company, Cunning Stunts, Matthew Child and Barbara Doherty, 2 Reel Company (Justin Case and Peter Wear), Forkbeard Fantasy, Sharon Landau, Friends Roadshow International, Jango Edwards, Cardiff Laboratory Theatre Company, Katie Duck, Lizzie, Bruce Lacey & Jill Bruce, Doc Shiels and Company, Orchard Theatre Company, and Robin's an Cruiso's Sensational Palace of (WHAT !? -- the only existing program has a hole punched through that last word.)

The Great Salt Lake Mime Troupe was led by Matthew Child and Barbara Doherty during much of 1979. The two made at least one trip to Australia, and also performed with Jodi Gilbert in Europe. They often played with actress/singer Sharon Landau, plus multi-instrumentalist Michael Moore (Gregg's brother) and drummer Michael Vatcher. These two musicians joined Available Jelly, and carried the band's name forward. After Barbara left the group, she relocated to Australia.

According to Matthew Child, the final performance by a group calling itself The Great Salt Lake Mime Troupe occurred in West Berlin during 1980, with the cast consisting of Katie, Georgio, Ernst Reijseger, and Michael Moore.

Amsterdam's Festival of Fools -- 1980

The most ambitious of all Festivals of Fools confronted a new decade.

The Festival was held at Meeuwenlaan, across the harbor from Centraal Station

Billed as an "International Theater Institute," it was administrated by the Shaffy, Paradiso, and Melkweg with tickets being sold at popular outlets throughout Amsterdam. The site itself was right on the water, very close to where *The Eye* houses Netherlands Film Institute in 2015.

Performers who were booked at the Festival of Fools in 1980 included:

(According to the program) Farid Chopel, Benito Gutmacher, Iris Scaccheri, Carlos Trafic, Hector Malamud, Graziella Martinez, The Murder Brothers, Sam Angelico and the Busby Berkleys, Triad Stage Alliance, Radeis, Eric de Volder, Het Etherische, Strijkers Ensemble, Parisiana, Ryamide op de Punt, INS Mannen Van Den Dam, Patrick Beckers, Guido Lauwaert, Friends Mobile Theatre, Les Enfants Du Paradis (Canada), Chatouille et Chocolat, Groupo Teatro Escambray, Germa Theater, Mobile Rhein Main Theater, F. J. Bogner, Volker Spengler, Bob Downes, The People Show, Stage Space Theatre Company, Air Design, Sharon Landau, Bloolips, Sheer Madness and Band, Footsbarn THeatre Company, Bob Kerr's Whoopie Band, Natural Theater, Chris Harris, IOU, Forkbeard Fantasy, The WeeWees, Two Reel Company, John Melville, Nola Rae, Theater Porquettas, Les Clown Macloma, Theatre De l'Unie, La F(d)ouce France, Manarf, Tuka Teatret, Studio K, El Hakqwati -- a Palestinian company from Israel, CFR, Piccolo Teatro Di Pontedera, Black Theatre Co-Op, Shusaku and Dorma Theatre, The Flint Brothers, Het Werkter, Bamsisters, Theathar Roma, Raffia, Ineke Cohen, Toneelgroep Baal, Mimetheater Termiek, Har Majesteit, Mekaniek, Fanfare St. Juttemis, Hauser Orkater, Carrousel, Stichting Dansprodukte, Dog Troep, Otto Van Den Meiden Puppet Theater, Waste of Time, ONK -- Theater Overal, De Vuilharmonie, Grifteater, Josef Van De Berg, Penta Theater, Varend Variete, Ka Theater, Rashomon, Wespetheater, Klein Pantomime Theater, Flup and Ju Dedrijf, Toneelgroup Centrum, Bevegingsgroep Bart Stuyf, Onafhankelijk Toneel, Teatr Osmego Dnia, Teatr Stu, Theatre National De Bucarest, Compania Alberto Vida, Divadlo Na Provazku, Praags Pocket Theater, Company of Crazy Mimes (CVOCI), Jango Edwards and the Pencilpeenie Circus, Katie Duck, Georgo Peugot and Jack Millet, Bob Carrol, Pigeon Drop, Steve Hanson, Pistol Theater, and Bumperto Bumper.

There was no 1981 Festival of Fools in Amsterdam

Among the many changes that took place around this time: Katie moved to Florence, Italy and ran a dance company named Grupo; Footsbarn Theater also attempted transferring their operations to Portugal;

Johnny Melville writes in 2014: *'81 was a good year for me.* **There was Festival of Fools in Copenhagen, Denmark**, *funded by the city and country with Jango and some French groups; In Aarhus, Denmark, there was another festival organised in similar ideas; Stockholm in 1981 -- Jordcirkus and a bunch of other Scandinavian groups; I worked with Earth (Jord) Circus on projects from then on -- met at various times through those two years doing cabarets and especially "Blood and Champagne," which premiered in Nancy, France during 1983.*

Amsterdam's Festival of Fools -- 1982

The program boldly announced Theater On The Street!

The 1982 Festival of Fools took place on nine stages around Amsterdam

Gielijn Escher played fast and loose with his Foolish Moons, and even signed this image.

FESTIVAL OF FOOLS AMSTERDAM 1982

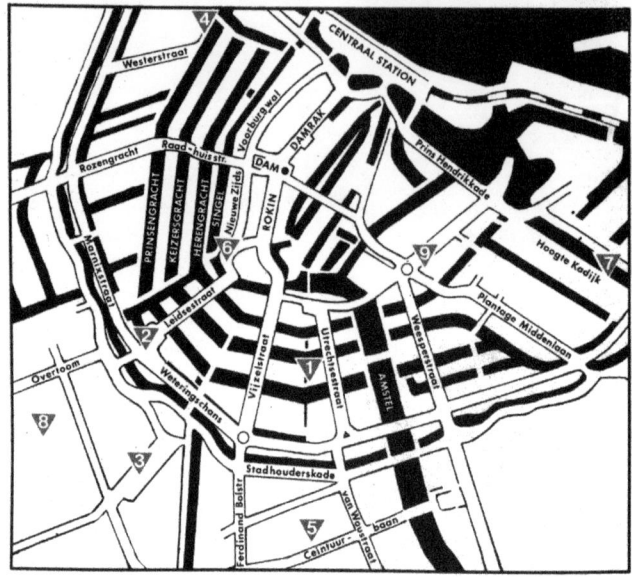

*1) Amstelveld; 2) Leidseplein; 3) Museumsplein; 4) Noordermarkt;
5) Sarphatipark; 6) Spui; 7) Varend Variete; 8) Vondelpark; 9) Waterlooplein.*

Performers who were booked at the Festival of Fools in 1982 included:

Rational Theatre, Radeis, Megafoon Fanfare, De Noufas, Bim, Martin, and Three, Sheer Madness, The Barneys (at this date Daniel Rovai and Miriam Smith), Pocket Theatre Company, Sharon Landau, Michael Banks, Corinne D'Cruz, Brian Popay, Pookiesnack-enburger, Motusse et Raillasse, Hen's Teeth, BAM Foundation, Blaguebolle, European Theatre of War, John Melville, Theatro Potlatch, Cabaret of Fools, Theatre Manarf, Teatr I Pokret, Shusaku and Dormatheater, Paul Clark, Flup Ju Bedrijf, Richie and the Losers, Werklos Theater, Theatro Nucleo, Paolo Passionato, Fanfare St. Juttemis, Het Kleine Flippen, ONK Theateroveral De Gees, Available Jelly, Flint Brothers, Pigeon Drop, D'Oude Stadt, Bamsisters, Trio Dynamo, Edwina Lee Tylor, Schmit 'ZZ Trauma Band, Teatro Real de Sevilla, Doc Maar, Dr. Hot and Neon Clone, Three Wheel Circus, Minus Delta T, Otto and Barnelli, Jordcirkus (Earth Circus) based in Sweden, with Chris Torch, Seherbentheater, Stoney Burke and the Fix-it-yourself Theatre.

In Search of ... Festival of Fools -- 1983

There was no festival in 1983, but a movie starring Jango Edwards and the Festival of Fools gang (narrated by Howard Hessman) was distributed via cable TV in the USA.

Proposed cover for a DVD release of Looking for Jango Edwards and the Festival of Fools (in) Amsterdam. Co-star Howard Hessman was from WKRP In Cincinnati on US television.

Looking for Jango Edwards and the Festival of Fools in Amsterdam:

Cast: Jango Edwards, Howard Hessman, Rick Parets, Johnny Melville, Peter Wear, Turne and Cindy Marler, Dr. Hot and Neon, Natural Theatre of Bath, Pigeon Drop. Music by Friends Band: Ted Bunting, Davey Norkett, Joe Braus, Hans Willem de Haan. Written by Rick Parets and Arthur Epstein; Additional material by Jango Edwards, Costume Designer -- Shirley Ferrini; Musical Director -- Ted Bunting; Additional compositions -- Davey Norket; Produced and Directed by Bertram van Meunster; Executive Producer -- Arthur Epstein.

Amsterdam's Festival of Fools -- 1984

The last incarnation of Amsterdam's Festival of Fools.

Four and twenty venues in and around and surrounding Amsterdam!

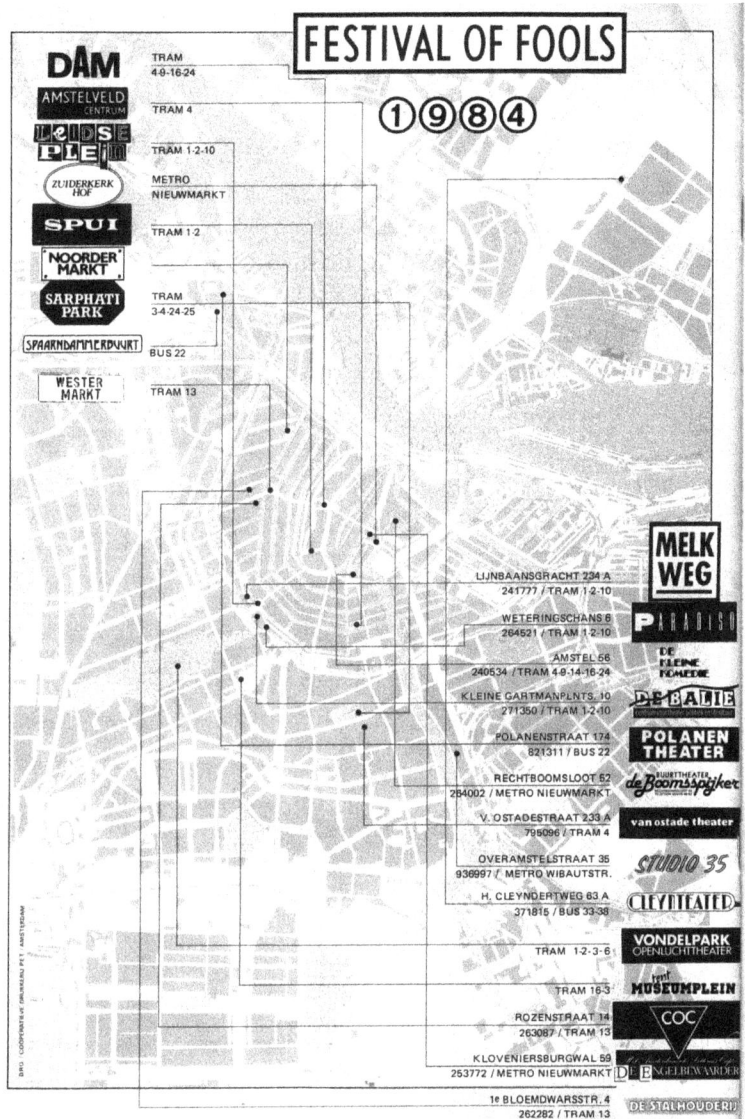

Festival of Fools sites in 1984:

Dam Square (The Dam), Amstelveld, Leidseplein, Zuiderkerk Hof, Spui (near today's ABC), Noordermarkt, Sarphati Park, Spaarndammerbuurt, Westermarkt, Melkweg, Paradiso, De Kleine Komedie, De Balie, Polanen Theater, De Boomsspgker, Van Ostende Theater, Studio 35, Cleyn Theater, Vondelpark Openlucht Theater, Tent Museumsplein, COC Rozenstraat, De Engelbewaarder, De Stalhouderij

Amsterdam's Festival of Fools did not go quietly into that goodnight ...

Performers booked at the Festival of Fools in 1984 included:

Alles Kids, Amazing Mendezies, Attic Theatre, Available Jelly, Avner the Eccentric, The Barneys, Blaguebolle, Boolips, Bob and Bob Jobbins, Vince Bruce Chrome, Cirque Scapin, Cirque du Trottoir, I Comnediant, Cultural Odyssey, Companie du Pot aux Roses, Confederacy of Fools, Desperate Men, Margaret Dolman, The Dutchies, Jango Edwards, Kindertheater Elleborg, Gebroeders Flint (Flint Bros.), Forkbeard Fantasy, Footsbarn Theatre, Dr. Hot and Neon, Roy Hutchines, Gardi Hutter, Neil Innes, Keefpleister, Krocht Theater, Bob Kerr's Whoopie Band, Sharon Landau, Tom Lebbink, Limited Company, Elaine Louden, The Malcolms, Marcelline Y Silvestre, Johnny Melville, John Mowatt Mime, Moving Picture Mime Show, No Panic, Off the Kerb Roadshow, Odehe Folkloric Troupe, Omelette Broadcasting Company (Peter Wear, Justin Case, Jim Sweeny, Steve Steen), Onde Kosa, Het Orkesje, ONK Theater Overal, Drs. P, Otto and Barnelli, Palfi, Paul en Joop Puppet Theater, Perspekt, Georgio Peugot and Jack Millet, Pigeon Drop, Pink (from NYC), Thomas Pinnock, Boleslav Polivka, Popla 84, Saperoco, Second Choices, Seeing Red Cabaret, Sheer Madness, Shusaku, Staunch Poets and Players, Tajphoon Tivoli (Sweden), Tickled Pink, Titanic and the Icebergs, Theatergroep Kip, Teatro Tascabile di Bergamo, Transparent Theater, Peter Wear, Webb Foote Productions, De Vente Binkies, Theatre des Manches a Balai, Teatro Nucleo, The Wee Wees, The Dutch, Wekin Uitvoering, Marc Zeegers and Jan Elbers, Zippo and Company, Theaterwekplaats, Abraxa Teatro, Goede Diel, Roots Anabo, Groupo Sportivo, Sisters of Mercy, Equaters, Kiem, and Culture Mambos. Pop stars: Psychedelic Furs, Shriekback, Lita Ford, Nick Lowe/Paul Carrack, and Prefab Sprout.

Clockwise from Upper Left: Steve Payne, Chip Bray, Marshall Erskine, and Stanley Haywood of Friends Roadshow, Lee Ross from Mime Troupe of America (Minnesota), and Jimmy Sernesky of the Great Salt Lake Mime Troupe/Available Jelly.

Afterword and Author's Notes

It took many fools to make those festivals, and many hands to make this light bit of work. Despite traveling rough, I managed to keep some of my own memorabilia over the years. As I began to post it online during the early millennium, people started sending me their own programs, photographs, and newspaper clippings by post and Internet, or allowing me to scan their own precious collections. These generous people include Johnny Melville, Ellen Beier, Paul Blackwell, Stuart Curtis, Karen Quest, Matthew Child, Mark Nelson, Gregg Moore, Peter Domela Nieuenhuis, Peter Wear, Jimmy Sernesky, Pat Droubay, Marion Onnekink, Cor Schlosser, Theatrical Institute Nederlands, Ted Van Zutphen, Ed Baker, Davey Norket, Marshall Erskin, and Suzette Bronkhorst -- all of whom contributed material used in this publication. Credits are gladly given whenever they are known.

The histories of the institutions and individuals that touch on this narrative are vast in number, and some of them are vastly important in modern artistic culture. LeCoq's circle of students and practitioners like Cirque de Soliel, Blue Man Group, and Julie (*Lion King*)Taymor have created the most commercially successful entertainment phenomena in history without much use of the word Mime in their publicity. The roots of the alternative Burning Man festival are also entangled with the International Mime Festival and Institute in 1974 via San Francisco's power-packed delegation. My online archive explores more paths through the decades, since the number of pages are finite in this book. Artists and groups like Footsbarn Theatre, Jango, Katie, and Johnny Melville still circle the globe teaching and performing in 2015.

The Melkweg and Paradiso continue to orbit the spaceport of Leidseplein, and the Open Air Theater still rocks Vondelpark every summer. Despite any protestation to the contrary, I see reflections of the Festival of Fools in the spectacular lunacy of Amsterdam's annual Uitmarkt, where bits of high art and low entertainment happen indoors and out, in fancy venues, in rows of fabric-covered booths alongside food stands, and commonplace picnic tables spread around the city.

Even though Amsterdam is turning 740 years old, the streets I knew have hardly changed compared to my old hometown of Salt Lake City, Utah. The old Centrum of Amsterdam echoes with the same vibrations for me, but Salt Lake's population increased by a factor of ten, and there is nothing like demolishing entire city blocks and altering whole downtown streets to alter the look of a town.

A fertile Dance/Ballet scene still exists in Utah's sprawling capitol city and talented students still seek the wider world, including Europe. I have seen work that is outstanding and would go over well with any audience across the Atlantic. I will also say the same about established companies who nourished Dance in the Intermountain West since I was a child growing up there. I'm also glad that Amsterdam has places like Bim Huis and OT301 to anchor potential bridges between countries and continents.

I revisited Europe sometime in every decade after I returned to the USA. Besides general travel and sightseeing, there were visits to Footsbarn's old stomping grounds in Cornwall, and a memorable two weeks at the Thirty-fifth Anniversary festival at their base in Central France. I even worked in Katie's summer workshops for a couple of years, shooting portable video, doing digital art, and sketching my fool head off on multiple occasions. I also made new friends among my students and on the streets of the outgoing city. Meeting my old mates who made their lives in Amsterdam were among the best experiences of all -- eating, drinking, swapping tales, and seeing what they did in various clubs, cabarets, and conservatories around the entertainment-hungry town. Other friends moved beyond the theatrical scene entirely, living full productive lives doing other endeavors.

Image of Italian poster courtesy of Matthew Child

Absent Friends

Stuart Curtis passed away suddenly in November of 2012 in Corvallis, Oregon. He generously contributed his personal account to the online saga in 2010 about making music with ace saxophonist Joe Levano at Friends Farm in 1975 . Mr. Levano had previously met the Friends Roadshow while he was with a band named "Bumbelee!" in Europe. We didn't know what that term meant when we first heard it, but we learned! Stuart returned to Europe in the Eighties, playing saxophone and clarinet in the orchestra for Hamburg's production of Andrew Lloyd Weber's "Cats" throughout its run.

In Memoriam -- George (courtesy of his friend Johnny Melville)

... Georgio Peugeot, the American clown was tragically killed in Switzerland on 17 August 2002 when his car was hit by a train. Georgio was a charming and gentle clown who started his performing days as a juggler in the 70s with the Salt Lake Mime Troupe from Utah. He was also part of that explosive Fools Scene which sprung out of Amsterdam and fathered the variety and street scenes of today. Soon after he developed a unique contact improvisation style with Jack Millet in the 80s. Georgio was also a proficient teacher, and later producer/director of various groups and events.

I first met Georgio in Barsham Fair, a medieval festival in England in 1975. I was performing at that festival with my group SALAKTA BALLOON BAND and on the first day there I noticed a large crowd enthusing round a juggler. Dressed in coloured overalls he had beautifully long reddish-blond hair which bounced on his shoulders in roll-up locks which a baroque wig-maker would have been jealous of. He was doing something I had never seen before - juggling a cauliflower, an apple and a peanut ... but here was Georgio innovating with 3 different sizes and weights, eating the apple as he juggled and when he finished that off he flipped the peanut high in the air and caught it perfectly in his mouth, the cauliflower perching on his neck. Over those days he also adopted a festival-partner: a 6 year old princess whom he integrated into his show: it was utter charm and it was funny too.

Over the years we met occasionally at festivals but it wasn't till the PALAZZO COLOMBI VARIETY 2001 that I actually worked with him when he urged me to perform in the show. I must say it was a very pleasurable experience. I worked with comedians and acrobats who were not only of the highest calibre, but also due to Georgio's acute sense of teamwork, were also generous and willing to share the limelight. He himself was open, fun, easy to work with and very serious about his comedy which all the great comedians are. He will be sorely missed by all, and my condolences go to his son and wife, THE COMEDY KIDS (in Freiberg, Germany), and all of us left in shock who knew him, worked with him and loved him. Losing clowns like Georgio the planet does not need right now.

www.ingramcontent.com/pod-product-compliance
Lightning Source LLC
Chambersburg PA
CBHW061813290426

44110CB00026B/2862